# The Tenant's Rights Manu
# The Essential Guide to the

#TenancyRights

# The Tenant's Rights Manual:
# The Essential Guide to the Law

#TenancyRights

Naomi Moore
Solicitor

Second Edition

Published 2017

Whilst the author has taken every care in preparing the material included in this work, any statements made as to the legal or other implication of transactions are made in good faith purely for general guidance and cannot be accepted for loss or expense incurred as a result of relying in particular circumstances on statements made in this work.

Copyright © 2017 Naomi Moore

All rights reserved. No part of this book may be reproduced, stored in a retrieval system, or transmitted in any way or by any means, including photocopying or recording, without the permission of the author.

The right of Naomi Moore to be identified as the author of this work has been asserted by her in accordance with the Copyright, Designs and Patents Act 1988.

**British Library Cataloguing- in- Publication Data**

A catalogue record for this book is available from the British Library.

ISBN-13: 978-1542505567
ISBN-10: 1542505569

# Foreword

The 2$^{nd}$ Edition of The Tenant's Rights Manual: The Essential Guide to the Law is updated with changes introduced by the Deregulation Act 2015, the Immigration Act 2016 and the Housing and Planning Act 2016.

The 2nd Edition provides tenants with up to date and current information on their tenancy rights to help them understand how to protect and enforce their rights.

At the end of each chapter is a Step-by-Step to walk readers through everything they need to know.

# Introduction

The first two chapters of The Tenant's Rights Manual: The Essential Guide to the Law is aimed primarily at tenants who are renting in the private sector and have an Assured Shorthold Tenancy. Subsequent chapters apply to Secure, Assured Tenants and Assured Shorthold Tenants.

This book is not a substitute for obtaining the services of a Solicitor and is not to be relied on. Tenants can find a list of Solicitors at: **www.lawsociety.org.uk.**

The relevant legislation contained in this book can be found at **www.legislation.gov.uk**

## Housing Law: Key Terms and Meanings

A reference guide to key terms within The Tenant's Rights Manual: The Essential Guide to Renting: Second Edition.

**Tenancy agreement**: The contractual agreement signed by a tenant and landlord which contains the key terms that governs the contractual relationship between the parties.

**Contract**: A legally binding agreement. A contract can be oral or written.

**Statute:** A Statute is an Act of Parliament that declares, proscribes, or commands something.

**Fixed term contract:** A contract which lasts for a specific period of time.

**Statutory Periodic term**: A contract for a specific period of time governed by statute.

**Break clause:** A term in a tenancy agreement which enables the landlord, tenant or both from ending the agreement early.

**Tenure:** The conditions under which land or buildings are held or occupied.

**Security of Tenure:** Statutory protection provided to tenure which restricts the rights of landlords to obtain possession of property.

**Assured Shorthold Tenancy:** Tenancies governed by the Housing Act 1988.

**Rent Act Tenant:** Tenancies governed by the Rent Act 1977.

**Secure Tenant:** Tenancies governed by the Housing Act 1985.

**Agricultural tenancy:** Tenancies governed by the Agricultural Tenancy Act 1988.

**Section 8 Notice:** Notice that is served on a tenant who is in breach of the terms of the tenancy agreement. *Section 8, Housing Act 1996.*

**Section 48 Notice:** A Notice that the landlord must serve on the tenant providing an address for the service of documents. *Section 48, Landlord & Tenant Act 1987.*

**Section 13 (Form 4) Notice:** A Notice of rent increase, *Section 13, Housing Act 1988.*

**Section 6 Notice:** Application referring a notice proposing a new rent under an assured periodic tenancy or agricultural occupancy to a Tribunal.

**Section 21 Notice:** A no-fault Notice that the landlord must serve on a tenant to obtain possession of an Assured Shorthold Tenancy.

**Notice to Quit**: A common law notice ending a common law periodic tenancy.

**Grounds for Possession:** Grounds for possession of property are set out in the statute that governs the tenancy agreement. A ground of possession is the reason that the landlord is seeking possession.

**No fault ground for possession:** The no fault ground for possession entitles the landlord to possession of the property even if the tenant has not breached a term of the tenancy.

**Prescribed information:** Information that must be given to tenants whose tenancies commenced on or after 1st October 2015.

**Tenancy Deposit scheme:** Government approved tenancy deposit scheme which protects a tenant's tenancy deposit. There are currently three in operation in England & Wales.

**Disrepair:** The legal definition of disrepair set out in Section 11, Landlord & Tenant Act 1985

**Condensation:** A combination of damp and mould caused by failure to adequately heat and ventilate property which results in condensation.

**Joint and several liabilities:** Joint tenants will be jointly and severally liable for the terms of the tenancy. E.g. if one party leaves both tenants will remain liable for all the rent due as per the terms of the tenancy.

**Express Term:** A written term that is contained within the tenancy agreement.

**Implied Term:** A term that if absent will be treated as though it should have been included in the tenancy agreement.

**House in Multiple Occupation:** A shared house that comes within the definition in *Section 254, Housing Act 2004*.

# Contents

| | Page |
|---|---|
| **1. Renting a Property in the Private Sector** | 1 |
| | |
| 1.1. Finding a property to rent | 1 |
| 1.2. Regulation of Estate and Letting Agents | 2 |
| 1.3. Viewing a new property: The tenant's checklist | 11 |
| 1.4. Holding Deposit | 12 |
| 1.5. Letting Agent fees & charges | 13 |
| 1.6. Client Money Protection | 16 |
| 1.7. The Tenancy Agreement | 19 |
| 1.8. Right to Rent | 21 |
| 1.9. Prescribed Information (How to Rent Guide) | 31 |
| 1.10. Gas Safety Check | 34 |
| 1.11. Energy Performance Certificate | 40 |
| 1.12. Property Inventories | 43 |
| 1.13. Professional cleaning | 45 |
| 1.14. Household contents insurance | 46 |
| | |
| **2. The Tenancy Deposit Scheme** | 47 |
| | |
| 2.1. Background to the Tenancy Deposit Scheme | 47 |
| 2.2. The Tenancy Deposit Schemes | 48 |
| 2.3. Tenancy Deposit Requirements | 49 |
| 2.4. Prescribed Information | 53 |
| 2.5. Initial requirements of the Tenancy Deposit Scheme | 60 |
| 2.6. Rent in advance or a tenancy deposit? | 61 |

| | |
|---|---|
| 2.7. Court Proceedings relating to tenancy deposits | 61 |
| 2.8. Penalties | 63 |
| 2.9. Return of the Tenancy Deposit | 65 |
| 2.10. Disputes over the return of the tenancy deposit | 66 |
| 2.11. STEP BY STEP GUIDE | 74 |

## 3. Harassment and Illegal Eviction — 79

| | |
|---|---|
| 3.1. Protection from Eviction Act 1977 | 80 |
| 3.2. Protection from Harassment 1997 | 85 |
| 3.3. Exclusions: Tenancies excluded from the Protection from Eviction Act 1977 | 90 |
| 3.4. Remedies: Action the tenant can take against harassment/Illegal eviction | 97 |
| 3.5. Reinstatement in the property | 101 |
| 3.6. Action a tenant can take if they have been illegally evicted | 104 |
| 3.7. Damages | 115 |
| 3.8. Landlord Defences | 117 |
| 3.9. STEP BY STEP GUIDE | 121 |

## 4. Disrepair — 125

| | |
|---|---|
| 4.1. Disrepair: The Law | 125 |
| 4.2. Disrepair or Improvement? | 128 |
| 4.3. Duty to carry out repairs | 129 |
| 4.4. Notice of Disrepair | 130 |

| | |
|---|---|
| 4.5. What is a reasonable period of time | 131 |
| 4.6. Tenant's responsibility | 133 |
| 4.7. Fit for habitation | 134 |
| 4.8. Section 4, Defective Premises Act 1972 | 135 |
| 4.9. Environmental Protection Act 1990 | 139 |
| 4.10. Housing Health and Safety Rating System (HHSRS) | 148 |
| 4.11. Remedies (Action the tenant can take if the landlord is not carrying out repairs) | 151 |
| 4.12. Damages | 154 |
| 4.13. STEP BY STEP GUIDE | 157 |

## 5. HMO (Houses in Multiple Occupation)     161

| | |
|---|---|
| 5.1. Definition: Houses in Multiple Occupation | 161 |
| 5.2. Licensing of HMO | 178 |
| 5.3. Requirements of a HMO | 181 |
| 5.4. Management regulations under the Housing Health and Safety Rating System (HHSRS) | 182 |
| 5.5. Management of HMO (England) Regulations 2006 | 183 |
| 5.6. Inspection of a HMO by the Local Authority | 191 |
| 5.7. Enforcement Action by the Local Authority | 191 |
| 5.8. Disrepair in a HMO | 193 |
| 5.9. Penalties for failing to licence a HMO | 195 |
| 5.10. STEP BY STEP GUIDE | 201 |

# 6. Possession Proceedings 203

| | |
|---|---|
| 6.1. Rent Act Tenancy | 205 |
| 6.2. Secure Tenancy | 211 |
| 6.3. Assured Tenancy | 215 |
| 6.4. Assured Shorthold Tenancy | 217 |
| 6.5. Fixed TermTenancies | 220 |
| 6.6. Notices (to end the Tenancy) | 221 |
| 6.7. Section 8 Notice of Seeking Possession | 222 |
| 6.8. Notice to Quit (NTQ) | 224 |
| 6.9. Section 21 Notice Requiring Possession | 227 |
| 6.10. When will a Section 21 Notice be invalid | 231 |
| 6.11. Revenge Eviction | 234 |
| 6.12. Accelerated Possession Procedure | 236 |
| 6.13. Which Court? | 238 |
| 6.14. Pre- Action Protocol for Social Landlords | 239 |
| 6.15. Standard Possession Procedure Claims | 240 |
| 6.16. Defences | 241 |
| 6.17. The Hearing | 243 |
| 6.18. Court Orders | 244 |
| 6.19. Money Judgment | 245 |
| 6.20. Court Costs | 246 |
| 6.21. Extension of time: Exceptional Hardship | 246 |
| 6.22. After the Hearing | 248 |
| 6.23. Challenging the Possession Order | 249 |
| 6.24. Warrant of Eviction | 252 |
| 6.25. Fast Track Evictions | 253 |

## 7. Housing Benefit　　　　　　　　　　　259

| | |
|---|---|
| 7.1. What is Housing Benefit | 259 |
| 7.2. Eligibility for Housing benefit | 260 |
| 7.3. Ineligibility for Housing benefit | 264 |
| 7.4. Local Housing Allowance | 266 |
| 7.5. Discretionary Housing Benefit | 270 |
| 7.6. Challenging a Housing Benefit Decision | 270 |

## 8. Common Questions & Answers　　　275

## 9. Legal Aid　　　　　　　　　　　　　297

| | |
|---|---|
| 9.1. Legal Aid: Legal advice and assistance | 296 |

## 10. Annex

| | |
|---|---|
| Annex 1: Tenancy Agreement | 302 |
| Annex 2: Prescribed Section 8 Housing Act 1988: Notice of Seeking Possession | 307 |
| Annex 3: Notice to Quit | 313 |
| Annex 4: Notice Seeking Possession of a Property let on an Assured Shorthold tenancy | 316 |

# CHAPTER ONE

## Renting a property in the Private Sector

### 1.1. Finding a property to rent

The first step in searching for property in the private sector begins with contacting letting agents, searching the internet, newspaper adverts and asking friends and family.

### Letting agents

A landlord may use a letting agent to manage a property on their behalf. Lettings agents are based in estate agent offices and they deal with the letting of properties to tenants. Alternatively, a landlord will manage the property without the services of a letting agent.

The role of the letting agent is to do the following:

- Market the property on the landlord's behalf.
- Negotiate the terms of the tenancy agreement and rental value of the property.

- Instigate legal proceedings to obtain possession on the landlord's behalf.

The landlord may have a management agreement with the letting agent which will detail what responsibilities the landlord and letting agent will have in the management of the tenancy.

The landlord may have a maintenance agreement with the letting agent which states who the tenant should report disrepair to and who is responsible for arranging the inspection and completion of repairs.

### 1.2. Regulation of Estate and Letting Agents

When approaching an estate and/or letting agent the first thing the tenant should enquire about is whether the agent is a member of a professional body that regulates letting and estate agents. Members of the organisations that regulate estate and letting agents are required to sign up to certain standards of practice and a tenant will have access to an independent complaints procedure should things go wrong.

If a tenant has cause to complain about an estate agent/letting agent they should take the following steps:

1) Check that the estate / letting agent is a member of the schemes listed below.

2) Contact the applicable scheme and follow the published complaints procedure on the scheme website.

3) If the estate/letting agent is not a member of a regulatory organisation the tenant should determine if there are grounds to commence legal proceedings.

**Organisations that regulate Estate Agents:**

**National Association of Estate Agents**

The NAEA is the UK's leading professional body for estate agents. Their main functions include regulating, guiding and assisting property professionals across a wide range of disciplines.

**Address**: Arbon House, 6 Tournament Court, Edgehill Drive, Warwick, Warwickshire, CV34 6LG
**Telephone number**: 0844 387 0555
**Website**: www.naea.co.uk

## The Association of Residential Letting Agents

The Association of Residential Lettings Agents (ARLA) is a professional membership and regulatory body for letting agents and letting agencies in the UK.

**Address**: Arbon House, 6 Tournament Court, Edgehill Drive, Warwick, Warwickshire, CV34 6LG
**Telephone number**: 0844 387 0555
**Website**: www.arla.co.uk
**Twitter:** ARLA@arla_uk

## The National Approved Lettings Scheme

The National Approved Letting Scheme is an accreditation scheme for lettings and management agents which agrees to meet defined standards of customer service. The Scheme offers insurance to protect clients' money plus a customer complaints procedure offering independent redress.

**Address**: Tavistock House, 5 Rodney Road, Cheltenham. GL50 1HX

**Telephone number**: 01242 581712 Fax: 01242 232518

**Website**: www.nalscheme.co.uk

## The Property Ombudsman

The Property Ombudsman has the power to make awards of compensation for financial loss and/or aggravation, distress and inconvenience, where it is appropriate. The service is free of charge for the public.

**Address**: Milford House, 53-55 Milford Street, Salisbury, Wiltshire SP1 2BP

### Consumer Enquiries

**Telephone number:** 01722 333306

**Email**: admin@tpos.co.uk

**Case Management:** If your complaint has been taken forward for review: casesupport@tpos.co.uk

**Twitter:** Property Ombudsman@TPOmb

## The UK Association of Letting Agents: UKALA

The UK Association of Letting Agents represent the interests of letting and management agents in the UK, whilst also safeguarding the interests of both landlords and tenants.

Use the UKALA Agent Directory and follow the directions to identify local members.

## General Enquiries

**Address:** UKALA Executive, 3rd Floor, 22-26 Albert Embankment, London, SE1 7TJ
**Telephone number:** 020 7820 7900
**Website:** www.ukala.org.uk
**E-mail:** info@ukala.org.uk

## Property Redress Scheme

On the 1st October 2014, it became a legal requirement for all letting agents to sign up to one of the three Government approved property redress schemes.

The Property Redress Schemes give tenants of letting agents an escalated complaints procedure if they are unhappy with how their complaint has been handled by the letting agent.

The three Property Redress Schemes are operated by:
- The Ombudsman services
- The Property Ombudsman
- The Property Redress Scheme

**Ombudsman Services**

**Address:** Ombudsman Services: Property, PO Box 1021, Warrington, WA4 9FE
**Telephone number:** 0330 440 1634
**Fax:** 0330 440 1635
**Text phone:** 0330 440 1600
**Website:** www.ombudsmanservices.org

**The Property Ombudsman**

**Address:** Milford House, 53-55 Milford Street, Salisbury, Wiltshire SP1 2BP

## Consumer Enquiries

**Telephone number:** 01722 333306

**Email:** admin@tpos.co.uk

**Case Management:** If your complaint has been taken forward for review: casesupport@tpos.co.uk

**Twitter:** PropertyOmbudsman@TPOmb

## The Property Redress Scheme

**Address:** Ground Floor, Kingmaker House, Station Road, New Barnet, Hertfordshire, EN5 1NZ.

**Telephone number:** 0333 321 9418

**Website:** www.theprs.co.uk

**Email:** info@theprs.co.uk

## Regulation of Landlords

If the property is being let by the landlord the tenant can check if the landlord is a member of the National Landlord Association or a landlord accreditation scheme. There are several landlord accreditation schemes across England and Wales. Accreditation is a set of standards or a code relating to the management or physical condition of privately rented property. Landlords who join the scheme must abide by the standards and are accredited.

## The National Landlord Association

The NLA is the leading association for private residential landlords in the UK.

**Address**: 22-26 Albert Embankment, London, SE1 7TJ
**Telephone number**: 020 7840 8900
**Website**: www.landlords.org.uk
**Email**: info@landlords.org.uk
**Twitter:** NLA@nationalandlord

## Code of Practice for Residential Letting Agents

If a letting agent is a member of ARLA 'The Association of Residential Lettings Agents' and is Registered with the Property Ombudsman, the agent will be bound by the Code of Practice for Residential Letting Agents, effective from 1$^{st}$ October 2016.

The full Code which residential letting agents must abide by can be found at: www.tpos.co.uk

## SAFE: Safe Agent

On the 3rd September 2011, SAFE: Safe Agent Fully Endorsed was launched. Safe Agent is a reliable mark that lets landlords and tenants know that a firm will protect their money through a client money protection scheme (CMP). All firms registered with Safe Agent are part of a client money protection scheme which reimburses clients in the event of misappropriation of a client's funds.

There are several other client money protection schemes in the sector operated by NALS, ARLA/NFOPP, The Law Society and RICS to which agents voluntarily belong. Each scheme varies and tenants should contact their agent for full details of the scheme of which they are apart.

Tenants should look for the SAFE kite mark to identify Safe Agents.

On the 27th May 2015, it became a legal requirement under *Section 83(6), Consumer Act 2015* that all agents display on their website and in their offices, whether they are or are not a member of a client money protection scheme.

More information on Safe Agent is available at:

**Address:** PO Box 1174, Cheltenham, GL50 9TQ
**Telephone number**: 01242 801 848
**Website**: www.safeagents.co.uk
**Email**: info@safeagents.co.uk
**Twitter**: @Safeagent

## 1.3. Viewing a new property: The tenant's checklist

When viewing a property, a potential tenant should thoroughly inspect the condition of the property from the outset to ensure that they are satisfied with the condition of the property.

**Checklist**

- The heating system is operating
- Check all windows
- Check for any signs of mould and damp
- Signs of leakage: staining to walls and ceiling
- Operating extractor fans
- All kitchen units open and close properly
- Check all fixtures and furnishings
- White goods are in good working order
- Visit the property at least twice
- Operating smoke alarm installed
- Evidence of pests e.g. mice droppings

**1.4. Holding Deposit**

A letting agent/landlord may request that the tenant pay a holding deposit to take the property off the market so that other potential tenants cannot view the property.

The letting agent/landlord is required to provide the tenant with a contract which sets out if the holding deposit will/will not be returned if either the tenant or the landlord/letting agent do not go ahead with the booking.

The tenant should read the contract in full and ensure that they are happy with the terms of the contract as they will be bound by these terms.

**1.5. Letting Agent Fees & Charges**

Letting agents can impose the following fees and charges on the tenant when administering the tenancy:

- Referencing checks
- Credit checks
- Drawing up the tenancy agreement
- Administration fees
- Drawing up a property inventory

Letting agent fees vary and can range from £100 upwards. In some instances, these charges are non-refundable if the letting does not go ahead.

The Advertising Standard Agency (ASA) has made it a mandatory requirement that a letting agents compulsory fees and charges are displayed in their property advertisements alongside rental prices.

If letting agents can calculate additional fees in advance, these will be included with the quoted asking rent. If non-optional fees cannot be calculated in advance; because they depend on individual circumstances, then advertisements must clearly state the nature of these and how they will be calculated.

It is a legal requirement that letting agents' display their fees. *Section 83, Consumer Rights Act 2015:*

**83 Duty of letting agents to publicise fees etc**

*(1) A letting agent must, in accordance with this section, publicise details of the agent's relevant fees.*

*(2) The agent must display a list of the fees—(a) at each of the agent's premises at which the agent deals face-to-*

*face with persons using or proposing to use services to which the fees relate, and*

*(b) at a place in each of those premises at which the list is likely to be seen by such persons.*

*(3) The agent must publish a list of the fees on the agent's website (if it has a website).*

*(4) A list of fees displayed or published in accordance with subsection (2) or (3) must include—*

*(a) a description of each fee that is sufficient to enable a person who is liable to pay it to understand the service or cost that is covered by the fee or the purpose for which it is imposed (as the case may be),*

*(b) in the case of a fee which tenants are liable to pay, an indication of whether the fee relates to each dwelling-house or each tenant under a tenancy of the dwelling-house, and*

*(c )the amount of each fee inclusive of any applicable tax or, where the amount of a fee cannot reasonably be determined in advance, a description of how that fee is calculated.*

*(5) Subsections (6) and (7) apply to a letting agent engaging in letting agency or property management work in relation to dwelling-houses in England.*

If the letting agent breaches *Section 83, Consumer Rights Act 2015* the Local Authority will be responsible for enforcing the provisions of the Act against the letting agent.

The Local Authority has the power to take the following action:

- impose a financial penalty against the letting agent, *Section 87(3) Consumer Rights Act 2015.*

- determine the amount of the financial penalty however it cannot exceed £5000.00, *Section 87 (7) Consumer Rights Act 2015.*

**Legal Update**: In the November 2016 Autumn Statement, the Government announced that it will be banning letting agent's fees. As of the date of going to press no timetable has been set by the Government for the new law to come into effect.

**1.6. Client Money Protection**

Property agents are required to be a member of a

client money protection scheme. A client money protection scheme protects the client's money against the theft or misappropriation of the client's money by the member's owners.

The Housing and Planning Act 2016 has introduced *Section 133-135* which gives the Secretary of State the power to require a property agent to become a member of a client money protection scheme.

### Housing and Planning Act 2016, Section 133-135

*133 Power to require property agents to join client money protection schemes*

*(1) The Secretary of State may by regulations require a property agent to be a member of—*

*(a) a client money protection scheme approved by the Secretary of State for the purpose of the regulations, or*

*(b) a government administered client money protection scheme that is designated by the Secretary of State for the purpose of the regulations.*

*(2) The regulations may impose requirements about the nature of the membership that a property agent must obtain (for example, by requiring a property agent to obtain membership that results in a particular level of compensation being available).*

*(3) The regulations shall—*

*(a) require a property agent to obtain a certificate confirming the property agent's membership of the scheme;*

*(b) require the property agent to display or publish the certificate in accordance with the regulations;*

*(c) require the property agent to produce a copy of the certificate, on request, in accordance with the regulations.*

*(4) In this section—*

- *"client money protection scheme" means a scheme which enables a person on whose behalf a property agent holds money to be compensated if all or part of that money is not repaid in circumstances in which the scheme applies;*
- *"government administered client money protection scheme" means a client money protection scheme that is administered by or on behalf of the Secretary of State;*
- *"property agent" means—*
    - *(a) a person who engages in English letting agency work within the meaning of section 54, or*
    - *(b) a person who engages in English property management work within the meaning of section 55, other than a person who engages in that work in the course of the*

*person's employment under a contract of employment.*

## 1.7. Tenancy Agreement

A tenancy agreement is a legal binding contractual agreement which sets out the terms and conditions that the landlord and tenant must abide by. A tenancy can be written or oral. It is not a legal requirement that a tenant be provided with a written tenancy agreement.

***Annex 1*** *contains an example of an Assured Shorthold tenancy agreement. The tenancy agreement that the letting agent/landlord will provide the tenant with may contain less or more terms then the example given.*

If a tenant is not provided with a tenancy agreement they can make a written request to the letting agent/landlord requesting that they be provided with a written statement of any term of the tenancy which is not in writing and that the following details be provided:

- The date on which the tenancy began or the date the tenancy came into effect.

- The rent payable and the date that the rent is due.

- Any term relating to rent review; and:

- If the tenancy is for a fixed term, the length of that term.

Failure to provide this information following a formal request is an offence under:

*Section 20 A (4) of the Housing Act 1988 as introduced by s97 of the Housing Act 1996.*

*(4) A landlord who fails, without reasonable excuse, to comply with a notice under subsection (1) above within the period of 28 days beginning with the date on which he received the notice is liable on summary conviction to a fine not exceeding level 4 on the standard scale.*

If the tenancy was agreed orally the landlord is required by law to provide the tenant with a rent book as prescribed by *Section 4 and Section 5, Landlord and Tenant Act 1985.*

## 1.8. Right to Rent

The Immigration Act 2014 introduced the requirement that landlords and letting agents must check if a tenant has a right to reside in the UK, *Section 22, Immigration Act 2014*. If the tenant does not have a right to reside the landlord/letting agent will be committing an offence.

*Section 22, Immigration Act 2014*

*22 Persons disqualified by immigration status not to be leased premises*

*(1) A landlord must not authorise an adult to occupy premises under a residential tenancy agreement if the adult is disqualified as a result of their immigration status.*

*(2) A landlord is to be taken to "authorise" an adult to occupy premises in the circumstances mentioned in subsection (1) if (and only if) there is a contravention of this section.*

*(3) There is a contravention of this section in either of the following cases.*

*(4) The first case is where a residential tenancy agreement is entered into that, at the time of entry, grants a right to occupy premises to—*

*(a) a tenant who is disqualified as a result of their immigration status,*

*(b) another adult named in the agreement who is disqualified as a result of their immigration status, or*

*(c) another adult not named in the agreement who is disqualified as a result of their immigration status (subject to subsection (6)).*

*(5) The second case is where—*

*(a) a residential tenancy agreement is entered into that grants a right to occupy premises on an adult with a limited right to rent,*

*(b) the adult later becomes a person disqualified as a result of their immigration status, and*

*(c) the adult continues to occupy the premises after becoming disqualified.*

*(6) There is a contravention as a result of subsection (4)(c) only if—*

*(a) reasonable enquiries were not made of the tenant before entering into the agreement as to the relevant occupiers, or*

*(b) reasonable enquiries were so made and it was, or should have been, apparent from the enquiries that the adult in question was likely to be a relevant occupier.*

*(7) Any term of a residential tenancy agreement that prohibits occupation of premises by a person disqualified by their immigration status is to be ignored for the purposes of determining whether there has been a contravention of this section if—*

*(a) the landlord knew when entering into the agreement that the term would be breached, or*

*(b) the prescribed requirements were not complied with before entering into the agreement.*

*(8) It does not matter for the purposes of this section whether or not—*

*(a) a right of occupation is exercisable on entering into an agreement or from a later date;*

*(b) a right of occupation is granted unconditionally or on satisfaction of a condition.*

*(9) A contravention of this section does not affect the validity or enforceability of any provision of a residential tenancy agreement by virtue of any rule of law relating to the validity or enforceability of contracts in circumstances involving illegality.*

*(10) In this Chapter—*

- "post-grant contravention" means a contravention in the second case mentioned in subsection (5);
- "pre-grant contravention" means a contravention in the first case mentioned in subsection (4);
- "relevant occupier", in relation to a residential tenancy agreement, means any adult who occupies premises under the agreement (whether or not named in the agreement).

## What the Right2Rent requirements mean for tenants

Tenants will be required to provide the landlord and/or letting agent with original documents that proves that the tenant has a legal right to live in the UK. A definitive list of the documents that a tenant will have to produce is available in the "Right to rent document: A users guide:

https://www.gov.uk/government/publications/right-to-rent-document-checks-a-user-guide

The landlord can terminate the tenancy if the tenants are disqualified from renting in the UK by serving the tenant with a Notice to Quit.

The Notice must be in writing and must give the tenant 28 days to vacate the property

The Notice acts as Warrant of Eviction and the landlord does not need to obtain a possession order to evict the tenant.

**Offences: Landlords**

*Section 39, Immigration Act 2016* inserted *Sections 33A-33D* into the Immigration Act 2014 which governs the penalties and offences that a landlord/letting agent commits if they let a property to a tenant who does not have a right to reside in the UK.

Section 33A, Immigration Act 2014

*33A Offences: landlords*
*(1) The landlord under a residential tenancy agreement which relates to premises in England commits an offence if the first and second conditions are met.*
*(2) The first condition is that the premises are occupied by an adult who is disqualified as a result of their*

*immigration status from occupying premises under a residential tenancy agreement.*

*(3) The second condition is that the landlord knows or has reasonable cause to believe that the premises are occupied by an adult who is disqualified as a result of their immigration status from occupying premises under a residential tenancy agreement.*

## Offences: Agents

*(1) Subsection (2) applies to an agent who is responsible for a landlord's contravention of section 22 in relation to premises in England.*

*(2) The agent commits an offence if the agent—*

*(a) knew or had reasonable cause to believe that the landlord would contravene section 22 by entering into the residential tenancy agreement in question,*

*(b) had sufficient opportunity to notify the landlord of that fact before the landlord entered into the agreement, but*

*(c) did not do so.*

*(3) Subsection (4) applies where—*

*(a) a landlord contravenes section 22 in relation to a residential tenancy agreement relating to premises in England,*

*(b) the contravention is a post-grant contravention, and*

(c) a person acting as the landlord's agent ("the agent") is responsible for the post-grant contravention.

(4) The agent commits an offence if—

(a) the agent knows or has reasonable cause to believe that there has been a post-grant contravention in relation to the agreement, and

(b) neither of paragraphs (a) and (b) of section 26(6) applies in relation to the post-grant contravention.

(5) Subsection (4) applies whether or not the agent is given a notice under section 25 in respect of the contravention.

**Penalties for landlords**

33C Offences: penalties etc, Immigration Act 2014

(1) A person who is guilty of an offence under section 33A or 33B is liable—

(a) on conviction on indictment, to imprisonment for a term not exceeding five years, to a fine or to both;

(b) on summary conviction, to imprisonment for a term not exceeding 12 months, to a fine or to both.

(2) In the application of this section in relation to an offence committed before the coming into force of section 154(1) of the Criminal Justice Act 2003 the

*reference in subsection (1)(b) to 12 months is to be read as a reference to 6 months.*

*(3) If an offence under section 33A or 33B is committed by a body corporate with the consent or connivance of an officer of the body, the officer, as well as the body, is to be treated as having committed the offence.*

*(4)In subsection (3) a reference to an officer of a body includes a reference to—*

*(a)a director, manager or secretary,*

*(b)a person purporting to act as a director, manager or secretary, and*

*(c)if the affairs of the body are managed by its members, a member.*

*(5)Where an offence under section 33A or 33B is committed by a partnership (whether or not a limited partnership) subsection (3) has effect, but as if a reference to an officer of the body were a reference to—*

*(a)a partner, and*

*(b)a person purporting to act as a partner.*

*(6) An offence under section 33A or 33B is to be treated as—*

*(a)a relevant offence for the purposes of sections 28B and 28D of the Immigration Act 1971 (search, entry and arrest), and*

(b) an offence under Part 3 of that Act (criminal proceedings) for the purposes of sections 28E, 28G and 28H of that Act (search after arrest)."

(3) In section 35 (transitional provision) after subsection (3) insert—

"(4) References in this section to this Chapter do not include sections 33A to 33E (offences and eviction).

(5) Sections 33A to 33C apply in relation to a residential tenancy agreement entered into before or after the coming into force of section 39 of the Immigration Act 2016 (which inserted those sections into this Act).

(6) But sections 33A(10) and (11) and 33B apply only in relation to a contravention of section 22 which occurs after the coming into force of section 39 of the Immigration Act 2016."

(4) In section 36 (Crown application) at the end insert "or the landlord for the purposes of section 33A."

(5) In section 37(4)(a) (provisions in which references to the landlord are to any of them)—

(a) omit the "and" at the end of sub-paragraph (ii), and

(b) at the end of sub-paragraph (iii) insert—

**Defences**

Section 33B, Immigration Act 2014

*(4) But unless subsection (5) applies the landlord does not commit an offence under subsection (1) if—*

*(a)the premises are located in an area in relation to which section 22 is in force,*

*(b)the adult mentioned in subsections (2) and (3) is a limited right occupier, and*

*(c)the eligibility period in relation to that occupier has not expired.*

*(5) This subsection applies if the Secretary of State has given a notice in writing to the landlord which—*

*(a)identifies the adult mentioned in subsections (2) and (3), and*

*(b)states that the adult is disqualified as a result of their immigration status from occupying premises under a residential tenancy agreement.*

## Summary

A landlord will have committed an offence if the property is occupied (or the landlord knows or has reasonable cause to believe that it is occupied) by an adult who is disqualified from renting because of their immigration status and from occupying premises under a residential tenancy agreement.

An agent will have committed an offence if they knew or had reasonable cause to believe that the landlord had contravened Section 22, Immigration Act 2014. The agent will also have committed an offence if they had sufficient opportunity to notify the landlord of that fact before the landlord entered into the agreement, but did not do so.

## 1.9. Prescribed Information

A landlord of a tenancy that commenced on or after the 1st October 2015 must provide the tenant with the following prescribed information at the start of the tenancy, *Section 39, Deregulation Act 2015:*

*39 Requirement for landlord to provide prescribed information*

*After section 21A of the Housing Act 1988 insert—*
*"21B Requirement for landlord to provide prescribed information*

*(1) The Secretary of State may by regulations require information about the rights and responsibilities of a landlord and a tenant under an assured shorthold tenancy of a dwelling-house in England (or any related matters) to be given by a landlord under such a tenancy, or a person acting on behalf of such a landlord, to the tenant under such a tenancy.*

*(2) Regulations under subsection (1) may—*

*(a) require the information to be given in the form of a document produced by the Secretary of State or another person,*

*(b) provide that the document to be given is the version that has effect at the time the requirement applies, and*

*(c) specify cases where the requirement does not apply.*

*(3) A notice under subsection (1) or (4) of section 21 may not be given in relation to an assured shorthold tenancy of a dwelling-house in England at a time when the landlord is in breach of a requirement imposed by regulations under subsection (1).*

*(4) A statutory instrument containing regulations made under subsection (1) is subject to annulment in pursuance of a resolution of either House of Parliament."*

***Regulation 3, The Assured Shorthold Tenancy Notices and Prescribed Requirements (England) Regulations 2015*** requires the landlord or landlord's agent to give the tenant the following information at the start of the tenancy:

- the current version of the "**How to rent: the checklist for renting in England**" guide, as published by the Department for Communities and Local Government, that has effect for the time being.

The information may be provided to the tenant:

- in hard copy; or
- by e-mail.

The other prescribed information requirements include:

- A copy of a Gas Safety Certificate (See Section 1.8). ***Regulation 2 (b) The Assured Shorthold Tenancy Notices and Prescribed Requirements (England) Regulations 2015***

- A copy of an Energy Performance Certificate (See Section 1.9). *Regulation 2 (a), The Assured Shorthold Tenancy Notices and Prescribed Requirements (England) Regulations 2015*

The failure to provide the tenant with prescribed information at the start of the tenancy will mean that the landlord cannot serve the tenant with a Section 21 Notice.

### 1.10. Gas Safety Check

The landlord is legally required to carry out an annual gas safety check by a gas safe registered engineer. *Regulation 36 of the Gas Safety (Installation and Use) Regulations 1998.* The gas safety engineer should provide the tenant with a copy of the gas safety record once s/he has completed the gas safety record. A copy of the **Gas Safety Certificate** must be given to the tenant at the commencement of the tenancy and within 28 days of the annual check. A copy must also be retained by the landlord for 2 years.

There is no one standard record that registered engineers use and they can produce their own record providing it contains the relevant information. The information that the form should include is set out as follows:

**Landlord Gas Safety Record**

- The date on which the appliance or flue was checked.

- The address of the premises at which the appliance or flue is installed.

- The name and address of the landlord of the premises (or where appropriate his/her agent) at which the appliance or flue is installed.

- The description of and the location of each appliance or flue checked;

- Any defect identified.

- Any remedial action taken.

- Confirmation that the check undertaken complies with the requirements as stated below;

- Where a person performs work on a gas appliance he shall immediately thereafter examine; -

- The effectiveness of any flue.

- The supply of combustion air.

- Its operating pressure or heat input, or where necessary both.

- Its operation to ensure its safe functioning, and forthwith take all reasonably practicable steps to notify any defect to the responsible person and, where different, the owner of the premises in which the appliance is situated, or, where neither is reasonably practicable, in the case of an appliance supplied with liquefied petroleum gas, the supplier of gas to the appliance, or, in any other case, the transporter.

- The name and signature of the individual carrying out the check; and

- The registration number with which that individual, or his employer, is registered with Gas Safe Register.

**Warning Notice**

- The name of the registered engineer issuing the notice.

- The registration number of the registered business.

- The site address of where the unsafe situation was addressed.

- Date of issue.

- Landlord contact details; name, address where appropriate (or, where appropriate, his/her agent).

- The signature of the responsible person and date of receipt of the notice.

- The Gas Industry Unsafe Situations procedure risk clarification being applied by the engineer.

- Confirmation that appropriate "do not use" labelling has been applied.

- It should include the following wording as this is the legal obligation on the responsible person signing the warning notice:

1. The responsible person for any premises shall not use a gas appliance or permit a gas appliance to be used if at any time, he or she knows or has reason to suspect that it cannot be used without constituting a danger to any person.

2. For the purposes of Paragraph (1) the responsible person means the occupier of the premises, the owner of the premises and any person with authority for the time being to take

appropriate action in relation to any gas fitting therein.

## Action that can be taken if a tenant fails to provide access for a Gas Safety check

If a tenant refuses and/or fails to provide access for a gas safety check to be undertaken the landlord cannot use force to enter the property. The landlord must make several attempts to arrange an appointment to carry out the gas safety check. If access is not obtained after at least three attempts the landlord may apply for an injunction for access for a gas engineer to carry out the gas safety check. The landlord can ask the tenant to pay the Court costs of applying for an injunction.

## Action that can be taken against a landlord who fails to provide a gas safety record or undertake a gas safety check

If the landlord has failed to provide a tenant with a gas safety record or arrange for a gas safety check to be undertaken, the tenant should contact the Health and Safety Executive (HSE) who can give the landlord a formal caution and take them to court.

The tenant can make a complaint online to the HSE via form LGSR1 available at: www.hse.gov.uk

If the tenant requires further information about gas safety and the landlord's responsibilities further information can be found at: www.gassaferegister.co.uk

**1.11. EPC: Energy Performance Certificate**

The landlord/letting agent of the property is required to provide the tenant with an Energy Performance Certificate at the start of the tenancy.

Energy Performance Certificates (EPC) give information on how to make a property more energy efficient and reduce energy costs. An EPC is valid for ten years from the date of issue. An EPC contains the following information:

- Information on a homes' energy use and

carbon dioxide emissions.

- A recommendation report with suggestions to reduce energy use and carbon dioxide emissions.

- Information on a home's energy use and typical energy costs.

- A recommendation report with suggestions to reduce energy use and save money.

- Details of the person who carried out the EPC assessment.

- Who to contact to make a complaint.

If the tenant is not given an EPC, they should contact the trading standards department of their local council.

Trading standards officers have the power to issue a fixed penalty notice of £200 to the landlord of domestic properties where an EPC is not provided.

On the 9th January 2013, the Government introduced legislation (Energy Performance of Buildings (Certificates and Inspections) (England and Wales)(Amendment) Regulations 2012) which means that a landlord/letting agent is required to do the following when letting a property to a prospective tenant:

- An EPC is required whenever a building is sold, constructed or rented out.

- It is the responsibility of the landlord to ensure that a prospective tenant has been provided with a copy of the EPC.

- A copy of the EPC should be given to a prospective tenant at the start of the tenancy.

- The EPC must be provided free of charge.

- Where a prospective tenant registers an interest in a property (by arranging a viewing or requesting further details), the landlord must make sure a copy of the properties EPC is available to them.

- There is no requirement to display the full certificate but where there is adequate space, the advertisement should show the A-G graph. If this is not possible the advertisement should include the actual EPC rating of the property.

- All sales or lettings advertisements in the commercial media (newspaper, internet, magazines, written material produced by landlord's/estate agents that describes the property being offered) should show the EPC rating of the property being advertised.

**1.12. Property Inventories**

At the start of the tenancy the landlord/ letting agent is required to take an inventory of the property with a schedule of the condition of furnished and/or unfurnished property before letting it out to potential tenants. A property inventory lists all the items in the property and the current condition of the items and the property at the time of the property being let.

The inventory should be taken with the tenant present at the time so that they can sign their agreement to the condition of the property as listed on the inventory.

At the end of the tenancy the landlord should perform a check out inventory with the tenant in attendance using the check in inventory as a cross-reference guide. Tenants should be advised that if the landlord fails to do a check in inventory at the start of the tenancy it will be difficult for the landlord to establish liability at the end of the tenancy and claim that the tenant is liable for any damage to the property.

If the tenant disputes the contents of the inventory and/or the landlord states that they will make deductions from the tenancy deposit due to damage to the property, the tenant can raise a dispute with the tenancy deposit scheme that holds the tenancy deposit. (See Chapter 2, Section 2.13 for more information on tenancy deposit disputes).

**1.13. Professional cleaning**

Landlords and/or letting agents will often charge tenants a professional cleaning fee at the end of the tenancy. However, they may not always be entitled to do so and a tenant is advised to check their tenancy agreement to check if the charge is legally enforceable.

The tenant should check if the tenancy agreement contains a clause about fees payable for the professional clean of the property when the tenancy ends. If the tenancy agreement is silent on cleaning charges the term is not enforceable by the landlord at the end of the tenancy as it did not form part of the original contract. If there is a term in the contract which states that the tenant is responsible for professionally cleaning the flat, the landlord will be able to enforce this term and charge the tenant for the service. In these cases, the tenant could seek to negotiate on these costs especially if they can clean the flat to the standard of a professional clean.

## 1.14. Household Contents insurance

A tenant is advised to take out housing contents insurance as the landlord's insurance will not provide insurance cover for the tenant's personal possessions in the event of accidental damage, fire and theft.

# CHAPTER TWO

# The Tenancy Deposit Scheme

**Introduction**

A private landlord must protect a tenant's tenancy deposit in a Government approved tenancy deposit scheme if the tenant has an Assured Shorthold Tenancy which started on or after the 6$^{th}$ April 2007. A tenancy deposit is typically the equivalent sum of 4-6 weeks rent which will act as a security against damage to the property caused by the tenant.

**2.1. Background to the Tenancy Deposit Scheme**

As of the 6$^{th}$ April 2007, all tenancy deposits taken in relation to Assured Shorthold tenancies must be put into a tenancy deposit scheme and the tenant must be provided with prescribed information about the scheme within 30 days of the landlord/letting agent receiving the tenancy deposit. The tenancy deposit rules are governed by *Section 212-215, Housing Act 2004*.

## 2.2. The Tenancy Deposit Schemes

There are three tenancy deposit schemes in operation in England & Wales. The schemes operate an **Insured** and/or **Custodial** Scheme.

**Insured Scheme**: The landlord/letting agent retains the deposit and pays the scheme a fee to protect the deposit.

**Custodial Scheme**: The tenancy deposit is held by the scheme and paid back to the tenant when they leave the property.

1. **Deposit Protection Service (DPS)**

    The DPS operates an Insured and Custodial scheme.

    **Website:** www.depositprotection.com
    **Tel no:** 0330 303 0030
    **Twitter:** @The_DPS

2. **My Deposits**

The MyDeposit Tenancy Deposit Scheme operates an Insured and Custodial scheme.

**Website:** www.mydeposits.co.uk
**Tel no:** 0333 321 9401
**Twitter:** @mydeposits

3. **Tenancy Deposit Scheme (TDS)**

The Tenancy Deposit Scheme operates an Insured and Custodial scheme.

**Website:** www.tenancydepositscheme.com
**Tel no:** 01844 262 891
**Twitter:** @TenancyDeposits

**2.3. Tenancy Deposit Requirements**

There are **three** requirements of the tenancy deposit scheme that must be complied with:

1)     The deposit must be registered with one of

the prescribed schemes within 30 days of receipt of the deposit.

2) The tenant and other relevant persons must be given a copy of the prescribed information within 30 days. The prescribed information must comply with the *Housing (Tenancy Deposits) Prescribed information) Order 2007*.

3) The tenant and other relevant persons must be provided with any leaflets provided by the scheme within 30 days of receipt of the deposit.

The requirements of the tenancy deposit scheme are governed by *Section 213, Housing Act 2004*.

**Section 213, Housing Act 2004: Requirements relating to tenancy deposits**

(1) *Any tenancy deposit paid to a person in connection with a shorthold tenancy must, as from the time when it is received, be dealt with in accordance with an authorised scheme.*

(2)   No person may require the payment of a tenancy deposit in connection with a shorthold tenancy which is not to be subject to the requirement in subsection (1).

(3)   Where a landlord receives a tenancy deposit in connection with a shorthold tenancy, the initial requirements of an authorised scheme must be complied with by the landlord in relation to the deposit within the period of 30 days beginning with the date on which it is received.

(4)   For the purposes of this section "the initial requirements" of an authorised scheme are such requirements imposed by the scheme as fall to be complied with by a landlord on receiving such a tenancy deposit.

(5)   A landlord who has received such a tenancy deposit must give the tenant and any relevant person such information relating to—

(a) the authorised scheme applying to the deposit,

(b) compliance by the landlord with the initial requirements of the scheme in relation to the deposit, and

(c) the operation of provisions of this Chapter in relation to the deposit, as may be prescribed.

(6) The information required by subsection (5) must be given to the tenant and any relevant person—

(a) in the prescribed form or in a form substantially to the same effect, and

(b) within the period of 30 days beginning with the date on which the deposit is received by the landlord.

(7) No person may, in connection with a shorthold tenancy, require a deposit which consists of property other than money.

(8) In subsection (7) "deposit" means a transfer of property intended to be held (by the landlord or otherwise) as security for—

(a) the performance of any obligations of the tenant, or

(b) the discharge of any liability of his, arising under or in connection with the tenancy.

(9) The provisions of this section apply despite any agreement to the contrary.

(10) In this section—

- "prescribed" means prescribed by an order made by the appropriate national authority;
- "property" means moveable property;

- *"relevant person" means any person who, in accordance with arrangements made with the tenant, paid the deposit on behalf of the tenant.*

## 2.4. Prescribed Information

*The Housing (Tenancy deposits) (Prescribed Information) Order 2007* sets out the Prescribed Information that must be given to tenants by the landlord/letting agent within 30 days of receiving the tenancy deposit.

**Prescribed information relating to tenancy deposits**

2. *(1) the following is prescribed information for the purposes of section 213(5) of the Housing Act 2004 ("the Act")—*

    *(a) the name, address, telephone number, e-mail address and any fax number of the scheme administrator of the authorised tenancy deposit scheme applying to the deposit;*

    *(b) any information contained in a leaflet supplied by the scheme administrator to*

*the landlord which explains the operation of the provisions contained in sections 212 to 215 of, and Schedule 10 to, the Act;*

(c) *The procedures that apply under the scheme by which an amount in respect of a deposit may be paid or repaid to the tenant at the end of the short hold tenancy ("the tenancy");*

(d) *The procedures that apply under the scheme where either the landlord or the tenant is not contactable at the end of the tenancy;*

(e) *the procedures that apply under the scheme where the landlord and the tenant dispute the amount to be paid or repaid to the tenant in respect of the deposit;*

(f) *The facilities available under the scheme for enabling a dispute relating to the deposit to be resolved without recourse to litigation; and*

(g) *The following information in connection*

with the tenancy in respect of which the deposit has been paid—

(i) The amount of the deposit paid;

(ii) The address of the property to which the tenancy relates;

(iii) The name, address, telephone number, and any e-mail address or fax number of the landlord;

(iv) the name, address, telephone number, and any e-mail address or fax number of the tenant, including such details that should be used by the landlord or scheme administrator for the purpose of contacting the tenant at the end of the tenancy;

(v) The name, address, telephone number and any e-mail address or fax number of any relevant person;

(vi) The circumstances when all or part

>
> of the deposit may be retained by the landlord, by reference to the terms of the tenancy; and
>
> (vii) Confirmation (in the form of a certificate signed by the landlord) that—
>
> (aa) the information he provides under this sub-paragraph is accurate to the best of his knowledge and belief; and
>
> (bb) he has given the tenant the opportunity to sign any document containing the information provided by the landlord under this article by way of confirmation that the information is accurate to the best of his knowledge and belief.
>
> (2) For the purposes of paragraph (1) (d), the reference to a landlord or a tenant who is not contactable includes a landlord or tenant whose whereabouts are known, but who is failing to respond to communications in respect of the deposit.

The tenancy deposit schemes provide pro-forma forms for Prescribed Information that can be given to tenants, however the forms vary in content and some schemes require the landlord to include information of the scheme in the tenancy agreement or by providing the tenant with a supplementary leaflet.

As each scheme differs a comprehensive guide is set out below to help tenants identify if the landlord has complied with the *Housing (Tenancy deposits) (Prescribed information) Order 2007.*

## MyDeposits Tenancy Deposit Scheme

If a tenancy deposit is protected in the MyDeposits tenancy scheme the tenant should be provided with the following documents by the landlord/letting agent:

- **Deposit Protection Certificate (DPC)**: The Deposit Protection Certificate contains information that the tenancy deposit is protected with MyDeposits and details of the deposit e.g. amount, tenant's name, landlord/letting agents name.

- **'Information for Tenants' Leaflet**: This leaflet should be given to the tenant with the Deposit Protection Certificate.

The following information is not contained within the Deposit Protection Certificate (DPC) or 'Information for Tenants' leaflet:

- The circumstances when all or part of the deposit may be retained by the landlord, by reference to the terms of the tenancy.

- Confirmation (in the form of a certificate signed by the landlord) that the information he provides is accurate to the best of his knowledge and belief;

- He has given the tenant the opportunity to sign any document containing the information provided by the landlord under this article by way of confirmation that the information is accurate to the best of his knowledge and belief.

The above information should be provided to the tenant either within the tenancy agreement or separately to ensure full compliance with the *Housing (Tenancy deposits) (Prescribed Information) Order 2007*.

## **The Deposit Protection Service**

If the tenancy deposit is protected in the Deposit Protection Service (DPS) tenancy deposit scheme the landlord/letting agent is required to provide the tenant with a template of the prescribed information which is available to download from the schemes website. The template must be given to the tenant with the following documents:

- The Deposit Protection Service Terms and Conditions.
- The Deposit Protection Service leaflet titled: A guide to tenancy deposits, disputes and damages.

## Tenancy Deposit Scheme (TDS)

If the tenancy deposit is protected in the Tenancy Deposit Scheme the tenant should be provided with the Prescribed information for assured short hold tenancies which is contained within the **Prescribed Information & Clauses for inclusion in terms of business, assured short hold tenancies (ASTs) and non-assured shorthold tenancies (non-ASTs) booklet.** This form is available to download from the Tenancy Deposit Scheme website.

The tenant should also be provided with the leaflet entitled **"What is the Tenancy deposit scheme?"**

### 2.5. Initial requirements of the Tenancy Deposit Scheme

The initial requirements of the tenancy deposit scheme must be complied with by the landlord in relation to the deposit within the period of 30 days beginning with the date on which it is received.

The initial requirements of the tenancy deposit scheme are such requirements *imposed by the scheme*. Each scheme has its own requirements therefore the landlord must ensure that they comply with the specific requirements of the scheme.

## 2.6. Rent in advance or a tenancy deposit?

Rent paid in advance will not be treated as a tenancy deposit and will not need to be protected in one of the tenancy deposit schemes if it has been paid to comply with the obligation to pay rent. If rent in advance is taken as a security against a tenant's obligations in respect of the tenancy, then it will be classified as a tenancy deposit.

## 2.7. Court Proceedings relating to Tenancy Deposits

If the landlord/letting agent does not comply with the tenancy deposit scheme requirements in *Section 213 (3) - (6) Housing Act 2004*, the tenant can make an application to the County Court and request that the Court makes one of the following orders under *Section 214 (3) - (4) Housing Act 2004*:

- Order the person who is holding the deposit

to repay it to the applicant.

- Order that the tenancy deposit be paid into a tenancy deposit scheme within 14 days from the date of the order.

- Order that the landlord repay the tenant the tenancy deposit plus an amount between 1-3 times the amount of the tenancy deposit amount.

## Section 214 (3) - (4) Housing Act 2004

(3)   The court must, as it thinks fit, either—

  (a)  order the person who appears to the court to be holding the deposit to repay it to the applicant, or

  (b)  Order that person to pay the deposit into the designated account held by the scheme administrator under an authorised custodial scheme, within the period of 14 days beginning with the date of the making of the order.

(3A)     the court may order the person who appears to the court to be holding the deposit to repay all or part of it to the applicant within the period of 14 days beginning with the date of the making of the order."

(4)       The Court must order the landlord to pay to the applicant a sum of money not less than the amount of the deposit and not more three times the amount of the deposit within the period of 14 days beginning with the date of the making of the order.

## 2.8. The penalties for non-compliance with the Tenancy Deposit Scheme

The penalties for non-compliance with the Tenancy Deposit Scheme are contained in *Section 215, Housing Act 2004*. If a landlord fails to protect the tenancy deposit and provide the tenant with prescribed information, the landlord will not be able to serve the tenant with a Section 21 Notice of Seeking Possession.

The exception is if the tenancy deposit has been returned in full, or returned less any agreed deductions before the Section 21 Notice of Seeking Possession is served.

## Section 215 Housing Act 2004, Sanctions for non-compliance

*(1) Subject to subsection (2A), If a tenancy deposit has been paid in connection with a shorthold tenancy, no section 21 notice may be given in relation to the tenancy at a time when—*

*(a) the deposit is not being held in accordance with an authorised scheme, or*

*(b) section 213(3) has not been complied with in relation to the deposit.*

*(2) Subject to subsection (2A), If section 213(6) is not complied with in relation to a deposit given in connection with a shorthold tenancy, no section 21 notice may be given in relation to the tenancy until such time as section 213(6)(a) is complied with.*

*(2A) Subsections (1) and (2) do not apply in a case where—*

*(a) the deposit has been returned to the tenant in full or with such deductions as are agreed between the landlord and tenant, or*

*(b) an application to a county court has been made under section 214(1) and has been determined by the court, withdrawn or settled by agreement between the parties.*

(3)  *If any deposit given in connection with a shorthold tenancy could not be lawfully required as a result of section 213(7), no section 21 notice may be given in relation to the tenancy until such time as the property in question is returned to the person by whom it was given as a deposit.*

(4)  *In subsection (3) "deposit" has the meaning given by section 213(8).*

(5)  *In this section a "section 21 notice" means a notice under section 21(1)(b) or (4)(a) of the Housing Act 1988 (recovery of possession on termination of shorthold tenancy).*

## 2.9. Return of the Tenancy deposit at the end of the tenancy

At the end of the tenancy the landlord is required to

do the following:

- return the tenancy deposit within 10 days of the tenancy formally ending and the tenant moving out of the property.

- If there is a dispute about the return of the deposit the tenant is entitled to raise a dispute with the tenancy deposit protection scheme provider that their deposit is protected in.

- The tenancy deposit schemes operate an adjudication process to help landlords and tenants resolve tenancy deposit disputes. The adjudication decision is non-binding, therefore if a tenant is unhappy with the decision they can issue a claim in their local County Court.

**2.10. Disputes over the return of the tenancy deposit**

The tenancy deposit may be retained by the

landlord in part/or in full at the end of the tenancy if the tenant breaches a term of the tenancy agreement which results in a financial loss to the landlord.

The most common disputes which affect the return of a tenancy deposit are: (the list is not exhaustive):

- The landlord claiming damages for damage to the property and redecoration.

- The landlord claiming for cleaning costs.

- Unpaid utility bills.

- Rent arrears.

**Evidence to defend a tenancy deposit dispute**

In tenancy deposit disputes the tenant should use the following documents to defend a claim brought by the landlord to make deductions from the tenancy deposit:

- *Tenancy agreement*

The tenancy agreement between the landlord and tenant will contain a term that the property should be in the same condition at the end of the tenancy, as it was at the start, and the tenant will be held liable for the cost of repair/replacement for any damage which exceeds fair wear and tear.

The tenant should ensure that they maintain the property in a tenant like manner so that the property is returned to the landlord in the same condition as when the tenancy commenced.

- *Check in and Check out inventory reports*

The inventory and schedule of condition at the start of the tenancy should detail the exact condition of each item/area. The inventory and schedule of condition will be used for comparison by the person completing the final inspection for the checkout report.

If the tenant disagrees with the contents of the

check-in/out process they should ensure that their comments are noted on the check-in/ out report.

The tenant should be given an opportunity to sign and date the check in and check out report to confirm their acceptance of the contents.

- *Photographic evidence*

The tenant should provide colour photographs of the property, specifying the date that the photograph was taken.

The photographs should be clearly marked showing the item/area which is in dispute.

The tenant should provide before and after photographs with a description of what the picture is showing.

Video evidence can be provided with a written explanation of what the video is showing.

- *Correspondence*

Emails/letters between the landlord/letting agent and tenant which provide evidence on what action either party has taken to resolve the dispute.

- *Invoices/receipts/estimates and quotations*

The landlord may produce invoices, receipts, estimates and quotations to show the cost incurred in respect of repair/replacement work being carried out. Receipts and invoices will carry more weight as they will show costs incurred. If an item cannot be replaced or repaired the landlord may be awarded a compensatory sum by the adjudicators at the tenancy deposit scheme/Court.

If the tenant has obtained estimates and quotes for the repair and replacement of items, these should be produced especially if the costs incurred by the landlord are excessively high in comparison and it can be shown that the costs incurred by the landlord are unreasonable.

- *Cleaning costs*

The cleanliness of the property should be made clear at the start and end of the tenancy and recorded by the landlord. The landlord will be required to provide invoices and receipts for work carried out by a professional cleaning contractor at the end of the tenancy.

The tenant is only required to return the property to the same state of cleanliness as at the start of the tenancy, after allowing for fair wear and tear.
It is arguable that the landlord is only entitled to deduct damages for cleaning which is above and beyond general wear and tear.

If the tenancy agreement makes no mention of cleaning costs then it will be more difficult for the landlord to deduct cleaning costs from the deposit if the tenant has cleaned the property at the end of the tenancy.

- *Rent arrears*

Account statements and /or bank statements which

show payments made to the landlord/letting agent will be required to defend the landlord's claim for rent arrears.

- *Utility claims*

If the tenancy agreement states that the tenant is responsible for the utility/council tax bills, then the issue of liability will be between the tenant and the local authority/utility provider. Therefore, the landlord will not be awarded any sum from the tenancy deposit unless the bills are not in the tenant's name or the landlord has had to pay any outstanding bills.

- *General wear and tear*

This is defined as "reasonable use of the premises by the tenant and the ordinary operation of natural forces".

It is also established legal principle that a landlord is not entitled to charge tenants the full cost of having any part of his property, or any fixture or fitting"

…put back to the condition it was at the start of the tenancy".

The landlord has a duty to act reasonably and not claim more than is necessary to make good any loss.

If any deduction is made from the tenancy deposit it should consider fair wear and tear and should not put the landlord in a better position financially or materially then they were at the start of the tenancy.

**Conclusion**

All the presented evidence will be considered by the tenancy deposit scheme adjudicator. The tenant is advised to provide all necessary evidence as detailed above to defend the landlord's claim to make deductions from the tenancy deposit.

## 2.11. STEP BY STEP GUIDE

If the tenant has not been provided with details of the tenancy deposit scheme that their tenancy deposit is protected they should take the following steps:

1. The three tenancy deposit schemes have a website that tenants can use to check if their tenancy deposit is protected. There is no central place to check all three schemes, so tenants will have to check each individually. Tenants will have to supply the property postcode, tenancy start date, tenancy deposit amount and name.

2. If the tenant's tenancy deposit is not protected then the tenant should send the landlord/ letting agent a Letter before Claim giving the landlord 14 days to place the deposit in one of the tenancy deposit schemes.

3. Upon the expiry of the 14-day period the

tenant should fill in and issue a Claim Form and Particulars of Claim at their local County Court. A Claim Form and Particulars of Claim Form is available from the local County Court or the Justice website: www.justice.gov.uk

4. A fee will be payable for filing the Claim Form and Particulars of Claim at Court. The cost of the application will vary depending on the value of the amount claimed. Information on fees can be found on the Justice website: www.justice.gov.uk. If the tenant is on a low income or in receipt of benefits they may be eligible for a fee remission which entitles them to a reduction or full waiver of the fee. The tenant must complete an EX160 to apply for a fee remission.

5. The Court will send a copy of the Claim Form and Particulars of Claim to the landlord/letting agent who will have a total of 28 days to file a Defence to the Claim.

6. If the landlord/letting agent defends the claim

an Allocation Questionnaire will be sent to the tenant and the landlord, who will both be required to complete it and send it back to the Court.

7. The case will be allocated to a case management track based on the value of the claim. There are three case management tracks that the Court can allocate a case to. The small track deals with cases up to the value of £10,000. If the case is worth more than £10,000 but less than 25,000 it is normally dealt with by fast track. Cases of value above £25,000 are normally considered more suitable for the multi-track. Once the case has been allocated to a case management track the Judge will order "Directions" which means that dates and times will be set by which certain tasks must be completed e.g. service of witness statements and disclosure of documents. The completion of these Directions will mean that the case is ready for the Judge to consider all the evidence at the final trial hearing.

8. The Judge will set a final hearing date to take place after all the directions have been complied with. At the final hearing both parties must attend Court and prove their case.

9. The Judge will decide on the outcome of the case at the final hearing.

10. The side that is successful is entitled to ask the Court to order that the loser pay the costs of bringing or defending the claim. These costs will usually be limited to fixed costs or costs that have been reasonably incurred (in small claims court cases).

# CHAPTER THREE

## Harassment and illegal eviction

### Introduction

This chapter is applicable to tenants who rent from private landlords and whilst relevant to tenants whose landlord is either a Local Authority or Housing Association, it is rare that the latter type of landlord would attempt to illegally evict or harass their tenants.

If a landlord wants to obtain possession of a Rent Act Protected, Secure, Assured or Assured Shorthold tenancy s/he must follow the correct legal procedure.

If the landlord (someone acting on the landlord's behalf) attempts to obtain possession without following the correct legal procedure and takes any action which amounts to harassment/illegal eviction the landlord (someone acting on the landlord's behalf) will have committed a criminal offence under the Protection from Eviction Act 1977.

## 3.1. Protection from Eviction Act 1977

*Protection from Eviction Act 1977*
*1. Unlawful eviction and harassment of occupier.*

    *(1)    In this section **"residential occupier", in relation to any premises, means a person occupying the premises as a residence**, whether **under a contract or by virtue of any enactment or rule of law giving him the right to remain in occupation** or restricting the right of any other person to recover possession of the premises.*

    *(2)    If any person unlawfully deprives the residential occupier of any premises of his occupation of the premises or any part thereof, or attempts to do so, he shall be guilty of an offence unless he proves that he believed, and had reasonable cause to believe, that the residential occupier had ceased to reside in the premises.*

    *(3)    If any person with intent to cause the residential occupier of any premises—*

> (a) to give up the occupation of the premises or any part thereof; or
> 
> (b) to refrain from exercising any right or pursuing any remedy in respect of the premises or part thereof; does acts calculated to interfere with the peace or comfort of the residential occupier or members of his household, or persistently withdraws or withholds services reasonably required for the occupation of the premises as a residence, he shall be guilty of an offence.
> 
> (3A) Subject to subsection (3B) below, the landlord of a residential occupier or an agent of the landlord shall be guilty of an offence if—
> 
> > (a) he does acts likely to interfere with the peace or comfort of the residential occupier or members of his household, or
> > 
> > (b) he persistently withdraws or withholds services reasonably required for the occupation of the premises in question as a residence, and (in either case) he knows, or has reasonable cause to

*believe, that that conduct is likely to cause the residential occupier to give up the occupation of the whole or part of the premises or to refrain from exercising any right or pursuing any remedy in respect of the whole or part of the premises.*

(3B) *A person shall not be guilty of an offence under subsection (3A) above if he proves that he had reasonable grounds for doing the acts or withdrawing or withholding the services in question.*

(3C) *In subsection (3A) above "landlord", in relation to a residential occupier of any premises, means the person who, but for—*

    (a) *the residential occupier's right to remain in occupation of the premises, or*

    (b) *a restriction on the person's right to recover possession of the premises, would be entitled to occupation of the premises and any superior landlord under whom that person derives title.*

*(4) A person guilty of an offence under this section shall be liable—*

*(a) on summary conviction, to a fine not exceeding £400 or to imprisonment for a term not exceeding 6 months or to both;*
*(b) on conviction on indictment, to a fine or to imprisonment for a term not exceeding 2 years or to both.*

*(5) Nothing in this section shall be taken to prejudice any liability or remedy to which a person guilty of an offence there under may be subject in civil proceedings.*

*(6) Where an offence under this section committed by a body corporate is proved to have been committed with the consent or connivance of, or to be attributable to any neglect on the part of, any director, manager or secretary or other similar officer of the body corporate or any person who was purporting to act in any such capacity, he as well as the body corporate shall be guilty of that offence and shall be liable to be proceeded against and punished accordingly.*

## **Summary**

It is a criminal and civil offence for the landlord/ letting agent to engage in any behaviour which:

- Interferes with a tenant's quiet enjoyment of their home.

- Unlawfully enters a tenant's property without permission.

- Interferes with the tenant's utility services.

- Changes the locks to prohibit the tenant from entering the property with the aim of denying the tenant rights over their property

These actions (non-exhaustive) will be regarded as an attempted/illegal eviction if the tenant feels harassed into leaving or leaves the property because of the actions of the landlord/ letting agent.

## 3.2. Protection from Harassment Act 1997

The Protection from Harassment Act 1997 governs the law on the prohibition of harassment by a landlord (or someone acting on the landlord's behalf) and the penalty for a landlord who harasses a tenant.

*Protection from Harassment Act 1997*
*1. Prohibition of harassment.*

(1)     *A person must not pursue a course of conduct—*

   (a)    *Which amounts to harassment of another, and*

   (b)    *Which he knows or ought to know amounts to harassment of the other.*

(2)     *For the purposes of this section, the person whose course of conduct is in question ought to know that it amounts to harassment of another if a reasonable person in possession of the same information would think the course of conduct amounted to harassment of the other.*

(3) Subsection (1) does not apply to a course of conduct if the person who pursued it shows—

(a) That it was pursued for the purpose of preventing or detecting crime,

(c) That it was pursued under any enactment or rule of law or to comply with any condition or requirement imposed by any person under any enactment, or

(c) That in the particular circumstances the pursuit of the course of conduct was reasonable.

## 2. Offence of harassment

(1) A person who pursues a course of conduct in breach of section 1 is guilty of an offence.

(2) A person guilty of an offence under this section is liable on summary conviction to imprisonment for a term not exceeding six months, or a fine not exceeding level 5 on the standard scale, or both.

### 3. Civil remedy

(1) An actual or apprehended breach of section 1 may be the subject of a claim in civil proceedings by the person who is or may be the victim of the course of conduct in question.

(2) On such a claim, damages may be awarded for (among other things) any anxiety caused by the harassment and any financial loss resulting from the harassment.

(3) Where—

    (a) in such proceedings the High Court or a county court grants an injunction for the purpose of restraining the defendant from pursuing any conduct which amounts to harassment, and

    (b) The plaintiff considers that the defendant has done anything which he is prohibited from doing by the injunction; the plaintiff may apply for the issue of a warrant for the arrest of the defendant.

(4) An application under subsection (3) may be

*made—*

> *(a) Where the injunction was granted by the High Court, to a judge of that court, and*
>
> *(b) Where the injunction was granted by a county court, to a judge or district judge of that or any other county court.*

*(5) The judge or district judge to whom an application under subsection (3) is made may only issue a warrant if—*

> *(a) The application is substantiated on oath, and*
>
> *(b) The judge or district judge has reasonable grounds for believing that the defendant has done anything which he is prohibited from doing by the injunction.*

*(6) Where—*
> *(a) The High Court or a county court grants an injunction for the purpose mentioned in subsection (3) (a), and*
>
> *(b) Without reasonable excuse the defendant does anything which he is prohibited from*

*doing by the injunction, he is guilty of an offence.*

(7)  *Where a person is convicted of an offence under subsection (6) in respect of any conduct, that conduct is not punishable as a contempt of court.*

(8)  *A person cannot be convicted of an offence under subsection (6) in respect of any conduct which has been punished as a contempt of court.*

(9)  *A person guilty of an offence under subsection (6) is liable—*

 (a)  *On conviction on indictment, to imprisonment for a term not exceeding five years, or a fine, or both, or*
 (b)  *On summary conviction, to imprisonment for a term not exceeding six months, or a fine not exceeding the statutory maximum, or both.*

## Summary

The Protection from Harassment Act 1997 creates a criminal offence which gives the Court the power to make a restraining order against the accused. A restraining order will prohibit a person from:

- Pursuing a course of conduct
- Which amounts to harassment of another and;
- Which he or she knows or ought to know amounts to harassment of the other.

The Protection from Harassment Act 1997 also creates a civil offence which gives the Court the power to award damages and order an injunction which prevents the accused from pursuing a course of action that amounts to harassment.

### 3.3. Exclusions: Tenancies excluded from the Protection from Eviction Act 1977

Unfortunately, the Protection from Eviction Act 1977 does not protect all tenants. If a tenancy falls within the definition below then the tenancy is an excluded tenancy and will not be protected by the Protection from Eviction Act 1977.

An excluded tenancy is defined in *Section 3A Protection from Eviction Act 1977*;

**Protection from Eviction Act 1977**

**3A. Excluded tenancies and licences**

(1)     Any reference in this Act to an excluded tenancy or an excluded licence is a reference to a tenancy or licence which is excluded by virtue of any of the following provisions of this section.

(2)     A tenancy or licence is excluded if—

    (a)     Under its terms the occupier shares any accommodation with the landlord or licensor; and

    (b)     immediately before the tenancy or licence was granted and also at the time it comes to an end, the landlord or licensor occupied as his only or principal home premises of which the whole or part of the shared accommodation formed part.

(3)     A tenancy or licence is also excluded if—

(a) Under its terms the occupier shares any accommodation with a member of the family of the landlord or licensor;

(b) immediately before the tenancy or licence was granted and also at the time it comes to an end, the member of the family of the landlord or licensor occupied as his only or principal home premises of which the whole or part of the shared accommodation formed part; and

(c) immediately before the tenancy or licence was granted and also at the time it comes to an end, the landlord or licensor occupied as his only or principal home premises in the same building as the shared accommodation and that building is not a purpose-built block of flats.

(4) For the purposes of subsections (2) and (3) above, an occupier shares accommodation with another person if he has the use of it in common with that person (whether or not also in common with others) and any reference in those subsections to shared accommodation shall be

*construed accordingly, and if, in relation to any tenancy or licence, there is at any time more than one person who is the landlord or licensor, any reference in those subsections to the landlord or licensor shall be construed as a reference to any one of those persons.*

(5)     *In subsections (2) to (4) above—*

    (a)     *"Accommodation" includes neither an area used for storage nor a staircase, passage, corridor or other means of access;*

    (b)     *"Occupier" means, in relation to a tenancy, the tenant and, in relation to a licence, the licensee; and*

    (c)     *"purpose-built block of flats" has the same meaning as in Part III of Schedule 1 to the Housing Act 1988; and section 113 of the Housing Act 1985 shall apply to determine whether a person who is for the purposes of subsection (3) above a member of another's family as it applies for the purposes of Part IV of that Act.*

(6) A tenancy or licence is excluded if it was granted as a temporary expedient to a person who entered the premises in question or any other premises as a trespasser (whether or not, before the beginning of that tenancy or licence, another tenancy or licence to occupy the premises or any other premises had been granted to him).

(7) A tenancy or licence is excluded if—

(a) it confers on the tenant or licensee the right to occupy the premises for a holiday only; or

(b) it is granted otherwise than for money or money's worth.

(7A) a tenancy or licence is excluded if it is granted in order to provide accommodation under Part VI of the Immigration and Asylum Act 1999.

(8) A licence is excluded if it confers rights of occupation in a hostel, within the meaning of the Housing Act 1985, which is provided by—

(a) the council of a county, [county borough,] district or London Borough, the Common Council of the City of London, the Council *of the Isles of Scilly, the Inner London Education Authority, [the London Fire and Emergency Planning Authority,] a joint authority within the meaning of the Local Government Act 1985 or a residuary body within the meaning of that Act;*

(b)  *A development corporation within the meaning of the New Towns Act 1981;*

(c)  *The Commission for the New Towns;*

(d)  *An urban development corporation established by an order under section 135 of the Local Government, Planning and Land Act 1980;*

(e)  *A housing action trust established under Part III of the Housing Act 1988;*

(f)  *Blank*

(g)  *The Housing Corporation . . .;*

(ga)  *the Secretary of State under section 89 of the Housing Associations Act 1985;*

(h) *A housing trust (within the meaning of the Housing Associations Act 1985) which is a charity or a registered social landlord (within the meaning of the Housing Act 1985); or.*

(i) *Any other person who is, or who belongs to a class of person which is, specified in an order made by the Secretary of State.*

(9) *The power to make an order under subsection (8)(i) above shall be exercisable by statutory instrument which shall be subject to annulment in pursuance of a resolution of either House of Parliament.*

## Summary

An excluded tenancy is a tenancy entered into on or after the 15th January 1989 and:

- The tenant shares the property with the landlord.
- The tenant shares the property with the landlord's family.

- The tenant is a former squatter.
- The tenancy was a holiday letting.
- The tenancy was granted to provide accommodation under Part VI of the Immigration and Asylum Act 1999.
- The tenancy is part of a hostel.

If a tenancy comes within the definition of an excluded tenancy, there will be no restriction on the right of the landlord to recover possession (subject to serving the tenant with a Notice to Quit) without obtaining a Court Order.

## 3.4. Remedies: Action the tenant can take against harassment/Illegal eviction

### Criminal proceedings

If the tenant is experiencing harassment or is at risk of illegal eviction the tenant should initially contact the police especially if the accused has used verbal threats and/or physical violence.

The tenant should also contact the Local Authorities

Tenancy Relations Officer (TRO) who must ensure as far as possible that private tenants are not harassed or illegally evicted.

The TRO has the power to bring criminal proceedings against the landlord (or someone acting on the landlord's behalf) in the Magistrates Court.

The Magistrates Court can impose a fine or six months' imprisonment or both if the individual in question has been found guilty of harassment and or illegal eviction. If the case proceeds to the Crown Court, then the landlord (or someone acting on the landlord's behalf) could be fined an unlimited amount and be sentenced to up to 2yrs in prison.

**Civil proceedings**

The tenant is entitled to call the police if the landlord (or someone acting on the landlord's behalf) has used violence to illegally evict the tenant. However, in the absence of violence the police will be reluctant to prosecute the landlord (or someone acting on the landlord's behalf) and will treat the matter as a civil case.

## Civil action the can take against the Landlord (or someone acting on the Landlord's behalf)

If the Police and/or Tenancy Relations Officer do not investigate an allegation of harassment/illegal eviction on the tenant's behalf, the tenant will have the option of commencing civil proceedings in their local County Court. The tenant is entitled to make an application for an Injunction and Damages (compensation) against the landlord (or someone acting on the landlord's behalf) to prohibit acts of harassment and attempts to illegally evict.

## Types of Injunction:

An injunction is an equitable remedy in the form of a court order that requires a party to do or refrain from doing specific acts. An injunction can be applied for to order that the landlord (or someone acting on the landlord's behalf) be prohibited from harassing the tenant and allow the tenant to return to/ enter their home. An injunction will be either interlocutory (interim) or a final injunction as detailed below:

## Injunction

An interlocutory (interim) injunction will prevent the landlord (or someone acting on the landlord's behalf) from harassing or attempting to illegally evict the tenant whilst proceedings are ongoing.

## Final injunction

A final injunction may be granted at the end of the trial when the factual dispute between the tenant and the landlord (or someone acting on the landlord's behalf) have been resolved. It will not normally be offered if damages is a better option. A final injunction will prohibit the landlord (or someone acting on the landlord's behalf) from taking any further unlawful action to obtain possession.

## Damages

The tenant may be entitled to claim financial

compensation for any acts of harassment and /or attempts to illegally evict. (Damages are considered in more detail at Section 3.7.)

### 3.5. Reinstatement in the property

If the tenant has been reinstated in the property following an unlawful attempted eviction, the tenant will still be able to start a claim in the local County Court against the landlord (or someone acting on the landlord's behalf) under the following causes of action:

### Causes of action: Tort

A Tort is a civil wrong. A tort is committed if the actions of another either intentional or unintentional has caused someone to suffer injury or loss. An individual who has suffered injury or loss is entitled to make a claim for damages to put them back in the position they would have been in if the act had not taken place.

## Trespass to goods

Any interference with another person's belongings is a trespass to goods. For example, if any of the tenant's items are destroyed or damaged the tenant will be entitled to bring a claim for trespass to goods. The tenant will require proof of damage, missing items and receipts to prove the value of goods.

## Trespass to property

The tenancy granted to a tenant entitles a tenant to possession of the premises to the exclusion of all others including the landlord. If the landlord (or someone acting on the landlord's behalf) enters the premises without permission, they are trespassing on a tenant's property. For example, it would be a trespass to property if the landlord changed the locks to the property and/ or entered the property when the tenant was not present.

## Causes of action: Breach of Contract

Once parties sign a (tenancy agreement) contract and one party does not do what they are contractually obligated to do, the other party can sue the defaulting party for breach of contract. The law will attempt to put the non-defaulting party back in the position they would have been in if the contract had not been breached.

## Breach of Quiet Enjoyment

Quiet enjoyment is an express and implied term of the tenancy agreement. Any conduct by a landlord (or someone acting on the landlord's behalf) which interferes with a tenant's freedom of action in exercising their rights as a tenant will be an interference with the tenant's quiet enjoyment of the property. E.g. disconnection of utilities, services, prohibiting entry to the property.

## Derogation from Grant

This is when the landlord uses the property in such

a way as to interfere with the tenant's use of the property for the purpose for which it was let. Where a landlord has taken steps, or granted rights to another party, which render the premises unfit or unsuitable for the purpose for which they were let, the landlord (or someone acting on the landlord's behalf) is said to have derogated from grant.

## 3.6. Action a tenant can take if they have been illegally evicted

If the tenant has been forced to move out by the landlord (or someone acting on the landlord's behalf), the tenant will be entitled to claim damages under *Section 27 and Section 28 Housing Act 1988*. The tenant will not be entitled to claim damages under *Section 27 and Section 28 Housing Act 1988* if they are reinstated back into the property / or if it was reasonable for them to return and they refused to do so. If reinstatement is offered and it is not reasonable for the tenant to move back into the property, the tenant will be entitled to claim damages under *Section 27 and Section 28 Housing Act 1988*.

A claim under *Section 27 and Section 28 Housing Act 1988* is an action brought under the Law of Torts.

**Section 27, Housing Act 1988. Damages for unlawful eviction.**

(1)   This section applies if, at any time after 9th June 1988, a landlord (in this section referred to as "the landlord in default") or any person acting on behalf of the landlord in default unlawfully deprives the residential occupier of any premises of his occupation of the whole or part of the premises.

(2)   This section also applies if, at any time after 9th June 1988, a landlord (in this section referred to as "the landlord in default") or any person acting on behalf of the landlord in default—

    (a)   Attempts unlawfully to deprive the residential occupier of any premises of his occupation of the whole or part of the premises, or

    (b)   Knowing or having reasonable cause to

*believe that the conduct is likely to cause the residential occupier of any premises—*

> *(i) to give up his occupation of the premises or any part thereof, or*
>
> *(ii) to refrain from exercising any right or pursuing any remedy in respect of the premises or any part thereof, does acts likely to interfere with the peace or comfort of the residential occupier or members of his household, or persistently withdraws or withholds services reasonably required for the occupation of the premises as a residence, and, as a result, the residential occupier gives up his occupation of the premises as a residence.*

*(3) Subject to the following provisions of this section, where this section applies, the landlord in default shall, by virtue of this section, be liable to pay to the former residential occupier, in respect of his loss of the right to occupy the premises in*

*question as his residence, damages assessed on the basis set out in section 28 below.*

(4) *Any liability arising by virtue of subsection (3) above—*

    (a) *Shall be in the nature of a liability in tort; and*

    (b) *Subject to subsection (5) below, shall be in addition to any liability arising apart from this section (whether in tort, contract or otherwise).*

(5) *Nothing in this section affects the right of a residential occupier to enforce any liability which arises apart from this section in respect of his loss of the right to occupy premises as his residence; but damages shall not be awarded both in respect of such a liability and in respect of a liability arising by virtue of this section on account of the same loss.*

(6) *No liability shall arise by virtue of subsection (3) above if—*

*(a)   before the date on which proceedings to enforce the liability are finally disposed of, the former residential occupier is reinstated in the premises in question in such circumstances that he becomes again the residential occupier of them; or*

*(b)   at the request of the former residential occupier, a court makes an order (whether in the nature of an injunction or otherwise) as a result of which he is reinstated as mentioned in paragraph (a) above; and, for the purposes of paragraph (a) above, proceedings to enforce a liability are finally disposed of on the earliest date by which the proceedings (including any proceedings on or in consequence of an appeal) have been determined and any time for appealing or further appealing has expired, except that if any appeal is abandoned, the proceedings shall be taken to be disposed of on the date of the abandonment.*

*(7)   If, in proceedings to enforce a liability arising by virtue of subsection (3) above, it appears to the*

*court—*

> *(a) that, prior to the event which gave rise to the liability, the conduct of the former residential occupier or any person living with him in the premises concerned was such that it is reasonable to mitigate the damages for which the landlord in default would otherwise be liable, or*
>
> *(b) that, before the proceedings were begun, the landlord in default offered to reinstate the former residential occupier in the premises in question and either it was unreasonable of the former residential occupier to refuse that offer or, if he had obtained alternative accommodation before the offer was made, it would have been unreasonable of him to refuse that offer if he had not obtained that accommodation, the court may reduce the amount of damages which would otherwise be payable to such amount as it thinks appropriate.*

*(8) In proceedings to enforce a liability arising by*

*virtue of subsection (3) above, it shall be a defence for the defendant to prove that he believed, and had reasonable cause to believe—*

    *(a)    that the residential occupier had ceased to reside in the premises in question at the time when he was deprived of occupation as mentioned in subsection (1) above or, as the case may be, when the attempt was made or the acts were done as a result of which he gave up his occupation of those premises; or*

    *(b)    that, where the liability would otherwise arise by virtue only of the doing of acts or the withdrawal or withholding of services, he had reasonable grounds for doing the acts or withdrawing or withholding the services in question.*

*(9)    In this section—*

    *(a)    "Residential occupier", in relation to any premises, has the same meaning as in section 1 of the 1977 Act;*

(b) "The right to occupy", in relation to a residential occupier, includes any restriction on the right of another person to recover possession of the premises in question;

(c) "Landlord", in relation to a residential occupier, means the person who, but for the occupier's right to occupy, would be entitled to occupation of the premises and any superior landlord under whom that person derives title;

(c) "former residential occupier", in relation to any premises, means the person who was the residential occupier until he was deprived of or gave up his occupation as mentioned in subsection (1) or subsection (2) above (and, in relation to a former residential occupier, "the right to occupy" and "landlord" shall be construed accordingly).

## Section 28, Housing Act 1988. The measure of damages.

(1) The basis for the assessment of damages referred to in section 27(3) above is the

*difference in value, determined as at the time immediately before the residential occupier ceased to occupy the premises in question as his residence, between—*

*(a) the value of the interest of the landlord in default determined on the assumption that the residential occupier continues to have the same right to occupy the premises as before that time; and*

*(b) The value of that interest determined on the assumption that the residential occupier has ceased to have that right.*

(2) In relation to any premises, any reference in this section to the interest of the landlord in default is a reference to his interest in the building in which the premises in question are comprised (whether or not that building contains any other premises) together with its curtilage.

(3) For the purposes of the valuations referred to in subsection (1) above, it shall be assumed—

(a) That the landlord in default is selling his

*interest on the open market to a willing buyer;*

(b) *That neither the residential occupier nor any member of his family wishes to buy; and*

(c) *That it is unlawful to carry out any substantial development of any of the land in which the landlord's interest subsists or to demolish the whole or part of any building on that land.*

(4) *In this section "the landlord in default" has the same meaning as in section 27 above and subsection (9) of that section applies in relation to this section as it applies in relation to that.*

(5) *Section 113 of the Housing Act 1985 (meaning of "members of a person's family") applies for the purposes of subsection (3) (b) above.*

(6) *The reference in subsection (3) (c) above to substantial development of any of the land in which the landlord's interest subsists is a reference to any development other than—*

*(a) development for which planning permission is granted by a general development order for the time being in force and which is carried out so as to comply with any condition or limitation subject to which planning permission is so granted; or (b) a change of use resulting in the building referred to in subsection (2) above or any part of it being used as, or as part of, one or more dwelling-houses; and in the Town and Country Planning Act 1990] and other expressions have the same meaning as in that Act.*

## **Summary**

A tenant will be entitled to bring a claim against the landlord (or someone acting on the landlord's behalf) in the following circumstances:

1. A landlord (or someone acting on the landlord's behalf) unlawfully deprives the tenant of the occupation of the whole or a part of the premises or;

2. A landlord (or someone acting on the landlord's behalf) attempts to unlawfully deprive the tenant of the occupation of the whole or a part of the premises and thus the tenant gives up occupation of the premises or:

3. A landlord (or someone acting on the landlord's behalf) does anything likely to interfere with the tenant's use, peace and enjoyment of their home or withdraws services reasonably required for the occupation of the premises as a residence and:

4. As a result, the tenant gives up accommodation and the landlord (or someone acting on the landlord's behalf) knew or had reasonable cause to believe that the tenant would give up occupation.

### 3.7. Damages

The tenant will also be entitled to claim damages if

they have been subjected to harassment and/or illegal eviction under the following heads of claim:

## General damages

General damages are designed to compensate for discomfort, loss of enjoyment, pain and suffering, shock, physical injury and inconvenience.

## Special damages

Special damages are designed to compensate for quantifiable losses e.g. the cost of alternative accommodation pending reinstatement to the premises and compensation for lost and damaged belongings.

## Exemplary damages

Exemplary damages are awarded to punish the landlord (or person acting on his behalf) and deter him from similar behaviour in the future.

Exemplary damages will be awarded if the landlord

has profited from the illegal eviction and what they have profited exceeds the compensation that may be awarded to a tenant.

**Aggravated damages**

The Court will award aggravated damages if the tenant has been subject to any form of violence, or aggravating factors which would entitle them to damages.

**3.8. Landlord Defences**

If a tenant brings a claim against the landlord (or someone acting on the landlord's behalf) the defence available to the landlord (or someone acting on the landlord's behalf) are as follows:

- If the landlord could prove or had reasonable cause to believe that the residential occupier (tenant) had ceased to reside in the premises (*Protection from Eviction Act 1977, Section 1(2)*). This is a statutory defence.

- The landlord has offered to reinstate the tenant back into the property and it is reasonable for the tenant to return.

- If the landlord offers to reinstate the tenant in the property before the tenant issues a claim in the County Court and the tenant unreasonably refuses, any damages the tenant may have been offered will be reduced. (Only applies to damages awarded under *s27 Housing Act 1988*).

- The tenant surrendered the tenancy e.g. handing in a notice, handing back keys, the landlord has accepted the tenants offer to settle the tenancy.

- The property has been re-let to a third party.

Any damages offered will be reduced in the following circumstances:

- Because of the conduct of the tenant as the former residential occupier.

- Or if the landlord offers reinstatement and it would be (or would have been) unreasonable for the tenant to refuse to accept. This offer must have been made before the tenant commenced legal proceedings.

**Paying legal fees**

The tenant may be able to obtain legal advice and representation to bring a private prosecution against the landlord (or someone acting on the landlord's behalf) if the Local Authority does not have a TRO or the TRO is reluctant to prosecute.

Free legal advice may be obtainable from the Citizens Advice Bureau or Law Centre® if the tenant is eligible for Legal Aid. Further details of these services can be found at:

- www.lawcentres.org.uk
- www.citizensadvice.org.uk

Alternatively, the tenant can find a Solicitor if they are not eligible for Legal Aid using the Law Society website: www.lawsociety.org.uk

If the tenant is eligible for Legal Aid they can find a Legal Aid Solicitor in there are on the legal aid finder website: www.find-legal-advice.justice.gov.uk

## **Summary**

If the landlord (or someone acting on the landlord's behalf) defends the claim using the defences set out above and is successful in satisfying the Court that the defences are proved, then the tenant's claim may not succeed. However, the success of a tenant's claim will depend on the facts of their case.

## 3.9. STEP BY STEP GUIDE

If the tenant wants to take civil action against a landlord (or someone acting on the landlord's behalf) to prevent harassment and/or attempts to illegally evict them, the tenant should take the following steps.

1. The tenant is required to complete and file an Injunction Application (Form N16A) at their Local County Court. An Injunction application (Form N16A) can be obtained from www.justice.gov.uk. An application fee is payable, however if the tenant is on a low wage or in receipt of welfare benefits they may be entitled to a fee remission. A fee remission will entitle an eligible person to a full/partial refund of the application fee. The fee remission application form EX160A can be obtained from the local County Court or www.justice.gov.uk

2. The Injunction Application must be accompanied with a witness

statement/affidavit setting out the contractual relationship between the tenant and the landlord and the behaviour of the landlord (or someone acting on the landlord's behalf) which justifies an injunction being ordered to prevent the action that the landlord is accused of.

4. The Injunction Application with an attached witness statement/affidavit should also include a Claim Form (Form N1) and Particulars of Claim setting out the cause of action. A Claim Form and Particulars of Claim can be obtained from the tenant's local County Court or www.justice.gov.uk. If the tenant intends to bring a claim for harassment the tenant should complete a Part 8 Claim Form (N208 Form).

4. A draft copy of the injunction order that the tenant is applying for should also be included. The draft injunction order should be completed on an Injunction Order (Form N16).

5. The Court will list a hearing for the same day that the application is filed if the application is made without notice due to the urgency in the case. If the Judge makes an order against the landlord (or someone acting on the landlord's behalf), a second hearing will be listed for a later date to allow time for the landlord (or someone acting on the landlord's behalf) to be served with a copy of the Injunction Order. At the second hearing the Judge will decide whether the Injunction should remain in operation until the outcome of the final hearing.

6. The case will be listed for a final hearing and the Judge will determine if the Injunction will remain in place in addition to deciding on any claim for damages.

# CHAPTER FOUR

# Disrepair

This Chapter applies to tenants in the private and social housing sector.

The landlord of residential property is responsible for remedying disrepair. This chapter will outline what is regarded as disrepair and what the tenant should do if the landlord fails to remedy disrepair in the property.

## 4.1. Disrepair: The Law

If a property is subject to disrepair there may be an *express term* contained in the tenancy agreement and/or a term will be *implied by statute, Section 11 of the Landlord and Tenant Act 1985* that the landlord is responsible for carrying out repairs within a **reasonable period of time** upon **receiving notice** of the disrepair from the tenant.

## **Section 11, Landlord & Tenant Act 1985**

The landlord has a statutory duty under *Section 11 Landlord and Tenant Act 1985* to keep in repair the structure and exterior of the dwelling and the water, gas, electrical and heating installations.

### *Section 11 (1) Landlord and Tenant Act 1985*

*In any lease of a dwelling-house, being a lease to which this section applies, there shall be an implied covenant by the lessor*

a) *to keep in repair the structure and exterior of the dwelling house (including drains, gutters and external pipes); and*

b) *to keep in repair and proper working order the installations in the dwelling- house for the supply of water, gas and electricity, and for sanitation (including basins, sinks, baths and sanitary conveniences but not, except as aforesaid, fixtures and appliances for making use of the supply of water, gas or electricity, and;*

c) *to keep in repair and proper working order the*

> *installation in the dwelling house for space heating or heating water.*

(3) *In determining the standard of repair required by the lessor's repairing covenant, regard shall be had to the age, character and prospective life of the dwelling- house and the locality where it is situated.*

## Express Terms

An Express Term is a term that is written into a contractual agreement. The parties to the tenancy agreement can agree to repair any reported disrepair which exceeds the duty to do so under *Section 11 Landlord and Tenant Act 1985*, however the tenancy agreement cannot state that the duty to complete repairs is anything less than stated in *Section 11 Landlord and Tenant Act 1985*.

## Implied Terms

An Implied Term is a term that will be regarded as contained within the tenancy agreement even if the term is not expressly stated. If the tenancy agreement is silent on who is responsible for repairs, *Section 11 Landlord and Tenant Act 1985* will be a term implied by statute into the tenancy agreement.

### 4.2. Disrepair or Improvement?

### Definition of Improvement:

An improvement is defined as any work which improves the appearance, quality and value of the property. A landlord will not be required by law to carry out any improvement work unless it is by way of an Improvement Notice.

### Examples of disrepair:

- Leaking roof/ceiling
- Broken/leaking toilet and wash hand basins
- No gas/heating/hot water
- Broken/leaking gutters
- Broken extractor fans
- Damp/mould caused by structural defects

## What is not disrepair?

- Broken kitchen units.
- Smashed windows (the landlord will be responsible for carrying out a repair if the damage has been caused by criminal activity which has been reported to the police).
- Broken cooker/washing machine- check the tenancy agreement to establish who is liable.
- Damp/mould caused by condensation (the landlord may be liable if the damp and mould is caused by a structural defect).
- Broken bed frames and mattresses - check the tenancy agreement to establish who is liable for replacement of these items

## 4.3. Duty to carry out repairs

The duty to carry out repairs is triggered once the disrepair is reported to the landlord/letting agent. If the landlord fails to remedy the disrepair within a *reasonable period of time* the tenant can commence court action against the landlord compelling the landlord to complete the repairs. The tenant can also claim compensation for any inconvenience, distress and suffering caused because of disrepair in the property.

## 4.4. Notice of Disrepair

The tenant must give the landlord notice of the disrepair as soon as reasonably practicable. The landlord will not be liable for remedying disrepair until s/he is put on notice of disrepair by the tenant.

Disrepair can be reported to the landlord/letting agent by the following methods:

- In person
- Telephone
- Letters
- Email

It is very important that the tenant keep a record of the dates/times of <u>all</u> instances of providing the landlord with notice of the disrepair. This will be important when the time comes to assess the value of any potential claim for compensation.

## 4.5. Reasonable Period of Time

Once the tenant provides the landlord with notice that there is disrepair in the property the landlord should arrange to inspect the property and complete the repairs within a reasonable period of time.

If the repairs are not completed within a reasonable period of time the tenant can commence further action against the landlord to get the repairs completed and potentially make a claim for compensation if they have suffered inconvenience, distress and suffering.

A reasonable period of time will be judged by a number of factors including the type and extent of the disrepair. For example:

A reasonable period of time to respond to emergency repairs such as an electrical failure, no gas supply or a large water leak would be 24 hours. A reasonable period of time for follow up works to put the property back into the state it was in prior to the disrepair will depend on how much work has to be done and the cost of the repairs. If the disrepair involves structural works, this may take more time to arrange and co-ordinate and the landlord would be justified in a taking longer to complete works.

**Examples of reasonable response times**:

**Urgent: Repairs within 24 hours**

Within the first 24 hours' steps should be taken to minimise the effects of the disrepair and then urgent works should be arranged to take place within 7 days.

- No gas or electricity supply
- Leaking roof

**Urgent: Repairs within 7 days**

- Gutter and overflow leaks
- Roof and chimney repairs
- Leaking toilets or cisterns
- Leaking taps

## Non- urgent: Repairs within 28 days

- Kitchen unit repairs
- Plasterwork
- Window or door frame adjustments

## 4.6. Tenant's responsibility

A tenant has an obligation to keep the property in a good state of repair. This obligation is normally stated as an express term in the tenancy agreement.

This means that the tenant is required to take reasonable care of the property and will be responsible for putting right any damage that they have caused to the property. At the end of the tenancy a tenant will be required to put the property back in the condition it was in at the beginning of the tenancy. If the tenant fails to take reasonable care of the property, the landlord may make deductions from the tenancy deposit at the end of the tenancy.

**4.7. Fit for habitation**

It is an implied term at common law that furnished accommodation be fit for human habitation at the start of the tenancy. If the property is not fit for habitation, then the tenant has the right to end the tenancy and move out upon providing the landlord with notice of their intention to end the tenancy.

The implied term only applies at the outset of the letting and it is not applicable when premises are let unfurnished.

Examples of unfitness for habitation

- Defective drains.
- Property is infested with statutory nuisances, rats, pharaoh ants, bed bugs.
- Hazards as defined by the Housing Health & Safety Rating System. (HHSRS) Housing Act 2004.

## What can the tenant do if the property is unfit for habitation?

If the tenant discovers that the furnished property is not fit for habitation at the outset of the tenancy, they have the option to leave the property and not be bound by the terms of the tenancy agreement. The tenant should act quickly as the longer that they stay and pay rent, they will then be deemed to have accepted the terms of the tenancy and the right to end the tenancy is lost.

The tenant should be advised that they are also entitled to bring a claim for breach of contract and claim compensation.

## 4.8. Section 4, Defective Premises Act 1972

The landlord has an obligation to take reasonable care to ensure that any person who might be affected by a defect (caused by disrepair) within the property are reasonably safe from personal injury or damage to the property.

If the tenant has suffered any personal injury because of disrepair in the property or because of the landlord's failure to carry out repair works to a reasonable standard the landlord will owe the tenant a duty of care in respect of the premises that the tenant occupies as set out in *Section 4, Defective Premises Act 1972.*

***Section 4 Defective Premises Act 1972, Landlord's duty of care in virtue of obligation or right to repair premises demised.***

(1) *Where premises are let under a tenancy which puts on the landlord an obligation to the tenant for the maintenance or repair of the premises, the landlord owes to all persons who might reasonably be expected to be affected by defects in the state of the premises a duty to take such care as is reasonable in all the circumstances to see that they are reasonably safe from personal injury or from damage to their property caused by a relevant defect.*

(2) *The said duty is owed if the landlord knows (whether as the result of being notified by the*

*tenant or otherwise) or if he ought in all the circumstances to have known of the relevant defect.*

*(3)   In this section "relevant defect" means a defect in the state of the premises existing at or after the material time and arising from, or continuing because of, an act or omission by the landlord which constitutes or would if he had had notice of the defect, have constituted a failure by him to carry out his obligation to the tenant for the maintenance or repair of the premises; and for the purposes of the foregoing provision "the material time" means—*

*(a)   where the tenancy commenced before this Act, the commencement of this Act; and*

*(b)   in all other cases, the earliest of the following times, that is to say—*
*(i) the time when the tenancy commences;*
*(ii) the time when the tenancy agreement is entered into;*
*(iii) the time when possession is taken of the premises in contemplation of the letting.*

*(4)   Where premises are let under a tenancy which*

*expressly or impliedly gives the landlord the right to enter the premises to carry out any description of maintenance or repair of the premises, then, as from the time when he first is, or by notice or otherwise can put himself, in a position to exercise the right and so long as he is or can put himself in that position, he shall be treated for the purposes of subsections (1) to (3) above (but for no other purpose) as if he were under an obligation to the tenant for that description of maintenance or repair of the premises; but the landlord shall not owe the tenant any duty by virtue of this subsection in respect of any defect in the state of the premises arising from, or continuing because of, a failure to carry out an obligation expressly imposed on the tenant by the tenancy.*

(5) *For the purposes of this section obligations imposed or rights given by any enactment in virtue of a tenancy shall be treated as imposed or given by the tenancy.*

(6) *This section applies to a right of occupation given by contract or any enactment and not amounting to a tenancy as if the right were a tenancy, and*

*"tenancy" and cognate expressions shall be construed accordingly.*

## Summary

To summarise under *Section 4, Defective Premises Act 1972* a landlord owes a duty of care to anyone who might be affected by relevant defects in the premises let by the landlord. The landlord is only liable for a relevant defect which results from a failure to carry out repair or maintenance work which the landlord was aware of or ought to have been aware of.

A tenant who has suffered any injury or the property they occupy has become damaged because of a defect or poor workmanship should contact a Solicitor for further advice and assistance.

## 4.9. Environmental Protection Act 1990

The tenant can commence action against the landlord if the property has any **statutory nuisances** which are **prejudicial to health**.

## Definition of statutory nuisance:

There is no specific definition of statutory nuisance other than matters which are prejudicial to health or a nuisance which interferes with a person's legitimate use and enjoyment of land.

The Environmental Protection Act 1990 and the Public Health Act 1936 lay down certain types of nuisances for which there is a statutory remedy. These include:

- smoke and fumes
- dust
- steam and smells
- piles of rubbish
- animals
- noise
- Cockroaches and rats (not mice)
- Pharaoh ants

## Definition of prejudicial to health

The term '**prejudicial to health or a nuisance**'

means something more than mildly annoying and would need to either be *injurious to health or likely to cause injury to health, or interfere with the normal use or enjoyment of property* to be classified as prejudicial to health.

Statutory nuisances are governed by *Section 79, Environmental Protection Act 1990.*

**Section 79. Environmental Protection Act 1990**
**Statutory nuisances and inspections**

(1)  *[Subject to subsections (1A) to (6A) below],* **the following matters constitute "statutory nuisances"** *for the purposes of this Part, that is to say—*

   (a)   *any premises in such a state as to be prejudicial to health or a nuisance*

   (b)   *smoke emitted from premises so as to be prejudicial to health or a nuisance;*

   (c)   *fumes or gases emitted from premises so as to be prejudicial to health or a* nuisance;

(d) any dust, steam, smell or other effluvia arising on industrial, trade or business premises and being prejudicial to health or a nuisance;

(e) any accumulation or deposit which is prejudicial to health or a nuisance;

(f) Any animal kept in such a place or manner as to be prejudicial to health or a nuisance;

(fa) any insects emanating from relevant industrial, trade or business premises and being prejudicial to health or a nuisance;]

(fb) artificial light emitted from premises so as to be prejudicial to health or a nuisance;]

(g) noise emitted from premises so as to be prejudicial to health or a nuisance;

(ga) noise that is prejudicial to health or a nuisance and is emitted from or caused *by a vehicle, machinery or equipment in a street*

*(h) any other matter declared by any enactment to be a statutory nuisance; and it shall be the duty of every local authority to cause its area to be inspected from time to time to detect any statutory nuisances which ought to be dealt with under section 80 below [or sections 80 and 80A below] and, where a complaint of a statutory nuisance is made to it by a person living within its area, to take such steps as are reasonably practicable to investigate the complaint.*

## What a tenant should do if they are experiencing a statutory nuisance in their property

A tenant affected by a statutory nuisance is advised to report it to the Local Authority if the landlord has failed to take steps to remedy the nuisance.

The Local Authority has a general duty under *Section 79, Environmental Protection Act 1990* to inspect their areas for statutory nuisances from time to time and a specific duty to take such steps as are reasonably practicable to investigate allegations of statutory nuisance.

Where a Local Authority is satisfied that a statutory nuisance exists, or is likely to occur or recur, it has a duty to serve an **abatement notice** on the landlord under *Section 80, Environmental Protection Act 1990*. The abatement notice may specify the works or steps which the Local Authority considers need to be undertaken for the nuisance to be abated. Alternatively, an abatement notice may simply require that the nuisance be abated and leave the means of doing so to the discretion of the person upon whom the notice was served. The recipient, in this case the landlord, of an abatement notice has a statutory right of appeal against the notice *(Section 80 (3), Environmental Protection Act 1990)*.

If a landlord is served with an abatement notice the landlord has a right of appeal to the Magistrates Court within 21 days.

If the landlord fails to comply with the requirements of an abatement notice the tenant should return to the Local Authority as the Local Authority has the power to take the following action:

- Prosecute the person responsible for the contravention or non-compliance.

- Issue proceedings in the High Court to secure the abatement, prohibition or restriction of the statutory nuisance.

- Carry out whatever works or action is necessary to abate the statutory nuisance and recover its reasonable costs in so doing.

## Complaint to the Magistrates Court

If a Local Authority decides that no statutory nuisance exists the tenant has the right to make their own complaint to the Magistrates' Court under *Section 82, Environmental Protection Act 1990.*

Before making a complaint to the Magistrates Court

the tenant must do the following:

- Give at least three days' notice to the person considered responsible for the nuisance of their intention to complain to the Magistrates' Court.

- The notice should provide details of the complaint and may be delivered by hand or by post.

- The tenant will be required to prove to the Magistrate, beyond reasonable doubt, that the nuisance they are complaining about amounts to a statutory nuisance.

- A date will be set for the hearing and the person about whom the tenant is complaining (person responsible for the nuisance or failure to remove the nuisance) will be summoned to Court.

- The tenant will be required to explain the problem and produce evidence of the disturbance.

- The tenant must give evidence and cross-examine their supporting witnesses to draw out their evidence. If the statutory nuisance is one of noise nuisance the neighbour causing the nuisance will be able to cross-examine the tenant and their witnesses and may produce their own evidence.

- If the tenant proves their case the Court will make an order requiring the nuisance to be abated, and/or prohibit recurrence of the nuisance. It also has the power at the time the nuisance order is made to impose a fine on the defendant (the landlord/ or neighbour) (currently up to £5,000).

- If this order is ignored further Court action will need to be taken; the tenant must therefore continue to keep records of nuisance in case it is necessary to return to Court.

- If the tenant fails to prove their case, the tenant may have to pay some of the defendant's expenses in coming to Court.

## 4.10. Housing Health and Safety Rating System (HHSRS) Housing Act 2004

The Housing Health and Safety Rating System is used to assess hazards in the property.

The Local Authority has the power to inspect premises which have been reported to them as suffering from defects which are a hazard under the Housing Health and Safety Rating System.

**What is a Hazard?**

There are 29 Hazards and they are set out in 32 pages in the Housing Health and Safety Rating System (HHSRS): Guidance for landlords and property-related professionals. A copy of the Guidance is available on the www.gov.uk website and can also be found using the link:

https://www.gov.uk/government/publications/housing-health-and-safety-rating-system-guidance-for-landlords-and-property-related-professionals

The categories of Hazards are: -

- Damp and mould growth, excess cold, excess heat, asbestos and MMF, biocides, carbon monoxide and fuel combustion products, lead, radiation, un-combusted fuel gas and volatile organic compounds.

- Crowding and space, entry by intruders, lighting and noise.

- Domestic hygiene, pests and refuse, food safety, personal hygiene, sanitation and drainage and water supply.

- Falls associated with baths etc., falling on level surfaces etc., falling on stairs etc., falling between levels, electrical hazards, fire, flames, hot surfaces etc., collision and entrapment, explosions, position and operability of amenities and structural collapse and falling elements.

If the property suffers from any of the following defects the tenant must do the following;

1) Report the defect to the landlord in writing.

2) Report the defect to the Local Authority (Environmental Health Department) if the landlord fails to remedy the defect within a reasonable period of time.

3) Once the tenant reports the defects to the Environmental Health Officer they should inspect the property to ascertain what hazards are present in the property.

**Action the Local Authority can take if Hazards are present in the property**

The Local Authority may decide to take the following action depending on the seriousness of the defects;

The Local Authority can act by:

- Issuing a **hazard awareness notice:** this warns the landlord that the Local Authority is aware of the problem.

- Giving the landlord an **improvement notice**, ordering the landlord to carry out certain repairs or improvements by a certain time.

- Ordering the **closure of all or part of a building or restricting the number of people** who live in the property.

- Taking **emergency action to do the repairs themselves** and reclaim the costs from the landlord.

- Making an order to **demolish the property**.

- **Buying the property from the landlord** under the compulsory purchase rules.

## 4.11. Remedies (Action the tenant can take if the landlord is not carrying out repairs)

If the landlord does not complete works to the property within a reasonable period of time upon receiving notice the following remedies are available to a tenant. Some of the options below will require

Court action and for this the tenant should consider instructing a Solicitor.

## Specific order for works

This is an order made by the Court requiring that specific works be completed by the landlord within a specific period of time.

## Injunction

This is an order made by the Court requiring the landlord to carry out emergency works to the property within a certain period of time.

## Interim injunction

This is an order made by the Court requiring the landlord to undertake works to the property pending the outcome of a final hearing on the landlord's liability for disrepair.

## Withholding rent

Although it is not advisable, a tenant who does decide to withhold rent until the landlord undertakes repairs should place the withheld rent in a separate account until the repairs have been completed by the landlord. The risk in withholding rent is that the landlord could commence possession proceedings on the grounds of rent arrears.

## Instructing tradesman to complete the work

The tenant can instruct a tradesman to complete the repairs if the landlord is failing to remedy the disrepair within a reasonable period of time, however the tenant is advised to obtain the landlord's permission to do so. The tenant will be required to obtain three comparative quotes and provide the landlord with copies of these quotes before instructing works to commence.

### 4.12. Damages

The tenant will be entitled to compensation (damages) if the landlord has failed to carry out repairs within a reasonable period of time. Compensation will be split into two headings;

### General damages

- discomfort and inconvenience/ loss of value of the tenancy
- injury to health/mental distress

### Special damages

- belongings damaged/ruined
- the cost of rectifying disrepair
- redecoration costs
- increased expenditure on heating
- cost of alternative accommodation

Damages will be calculated and can be claimed from the landlord once all the works have been completed. The tenant must prove that the landlord was liable for the disrepair and failed to carry out works within a reasonable period of time upon receiving notice of the disrepair.

## Calculating damages

The approach used to calculate how much **general damages** a tenant can claim for disrepair can be summarised as follows:

- During the period that the tenant remains in occupation of the property whilst it is in a state of disrepair, the calculation for the loss incurred which the tenant should be compensated for is the: *loss of comfort and convenience which has occurred as a result of the disrepair.*

- The question for the Judge is the monetary value of the discomfort and inconvenience suffered by the tenant.

## Compensation may be assessed in the following ways

The approach adopted by Judges to calculate compensation is:

1. Diminution (reduction) in the value of the property to the tenant calculated by reference to a proportion of the rent payable. Or:

2. An assessment of the discomfort and inconvenience suffered made without reference to the rent payable.

3. Judges may adopt a combination of both approaches to determine the amount of compensation that a tenant is entitled to.

## 4.13. STEP BY STEP GUIDE

If the landlord/letting agent has not taken any action to remedy disrepair the tenant should follow our Step by Step guide:

1. If the tenant instructs a Solicitor a Pre-Action Protocol letter will be sent to the landlord. A Pre-Action Protocol letter will notify the landlord of outstanding disrepair and provides the landlord with a reasonable time to inspect the property and remedy the disrepair.

2. Alternatively, a tenant acting without a Solicitor can send the landlord a Pre-Action Protocol letter. An example of a Pre-Action letter can be found in the CPR: Pre-Action Protocol for Housing Disrepair: http://www.justice.gov.uk/courts/procedure-rules/civil/protocol/prot_hou

3. If the landlord fails to inspect the property and prepare a Schedule of Works to remedy

the disrepair within 20 working days, a Solicitor may instruct a Surveyor to inspect the premises to determine what works the landlord is liable to complete and the best method to remedy the disrepair.

4. The landlord will be sent a copy of the Surveyor's report and will be given a reasonable period of time to undertake the work to remedy the disrepair. If the landlord fails to undertake the work then the Solicitor will instigate proceedings in the Local County Court requiring the landlord to complete the works and claim compensation for any loss, suffering and inconvenience suffered by the tenant.

4. If the works are urgent the tenant's Solicitor or if the tenant is acting as a litigant in person, may apply for specific performance or an injunction requiring works to be carried out immediately. The Court must be satisfied that the repairs are serious and life-threatening and that if the tenant were to

proceed to a full trial they would obtain the order they were seeking.

5. If the disrepair constitutes a statutory nuisance, the tenant should contact the Environmental Health Department (EHO) at their Local Authority. The EHO will inspect the property and if hazards are present they will serve the landlord with an appropriate notice. The notice gives the landlord 20 days to remedy the disrepair. If the work is not undertaken within 20 days, the EHO has powers to instigate action against the landlord.

6. If the landlord is a private landlord an alternative option to get works completed is for the tenant to obtain two competitive quotes from skilled tradesmen. The landlord should be provided with copies of the quotes and the tenant will be required to explain the reason for picking a tradesman. The tenant should advise the landlord beforehand that they will subtract the costs incurred from the rent due.

# CHAPTER FIVE

# Houses in Multiple Occupation

*Introduction*

A tenant who lives in shared accommodation, may live in accommodation which is classified as a House in Multiple Occupation (HMO). If the property comes within the definition of a House in Multiple Occupation, there are several statutory requirements and penalties that the landlord must abide by and will be subject to. This chapter identifies the landlord's obligations and duties to tenants who live in HMOs.

## 5.1. Definition: Houses in Multiple occupation (HMO).

The legal definition of a HMO is set out at *Section 77 and Section 254-259, Housing Act 2004.* A property will be classified as a HMO if it has the following features:

- The property has three floors or accommodates more than three tenants in single units who share kitchen and bathroom facilities.

- Occupied by 5 or more people, including children.

- Occupied by 2 or more households.

**Section 254, Housing Act 2004: Meaning of "house in multiple occupation"**

(1) For the purposes of this Act a building or a part of a building is a "house in multiple occupation" if—

    (a) it meets the conditions in subsection (2) ("the standard test");

    (b) it meets the conditions in subsection (3) ("the self-contained flat test");

    (c) it meets the conditions in subsection (4) ("the converted building test");

    (d) an HMO declaration is in force in respect of it under section 255; or

(e) it is a converted block of flats to which section 257 applies.

(2) A building or a part of a building meets the standard test if—

(a) it consists of one or more units of living accommodation not consisting of a self-contained flat or flats;

(b) the living accommodation is occupied by persons who do not form a single household (see section 258);

(c) the living accommodation is occupied by those persons as their only or main residence or they are to be treated as so occupying it (see section 259);

(d) their occupation of the living accommodation constitutes the only use of that accommodation;

(e) rents are payable or other consideration is to be provided in respect of at least one of those persons' occupation of the living accommodation; and

(f) two or more of the households who occupy the living accommodation share one or more basic amenities or the living accommodation is lacking in one or more basic amenities.

(3) A part of a building meets the self-contained flat test if—

(a) it consists of a self-contained flat; and

(b) paragraphs (b) to (f) of subsection (2) apply (reading references to the living accommodation concerned as references to the flat).

(4) A building or a part of a building meets the converted building test if—

(a) it is a converted building;

(b) it contains one or more units of living accommodation that do not consist of a self-contained flat or flats (whether or not it also contains any such flat or flats);

*(c) the living accommodation is occupied by persons who do not form a single household (section 258);*

*(d) the living accommodation is occupied by those persons as their only or main residence or they are to be treated as so occupying it (see section 259);*

*(e) their occupation of the living accommodation constitutes the only use of that accommodation; and*

*(f) rents are payable or other consideration is to be provided in respect of at least one of those persons' occupation of the living accommodation.*

*(5) But for any purposes of this Act (other than those of Part 1) a building or part of a building within subsection (1) is not a house in multiple occupation if it is listed in Schedule 14.*

*(6) The appropriate national authority may by regulations—*

(a) make such amendments of this section and sections 255 to 259 as the authority considers appropriate with a view to securing that any building or part of a building of a description specified in the regulations is or is not to be a house in multiple occupation for any specified purposes of this Act;

(b) provide for such amendments to have effect also for the purposes of definitions in other enactments that operate by reference to this Act;

(c) make such consequential amendments of any provision of this Act, or any other enactment, as the authority considers appropriate.

(7) Regulations under subsection (6) may frame any description by reference to any matters or circumstances whatever.

(8) In this section—
"basic amenities" means—
(a) a toilet,

*(b) personal washing facilities, or*

*(c) cooking facilities;*

*"converted building" means a building or part of a building consisting of living accommodation in which one or more units of such accommodation have been created since the building or part was constructed;*

*"enactment" includes an enactment comprised in subordinate legislation (within the meaning of the Interpretation Act 1978 (c. 30)*

*"self-contained flat" means a separate set of premises (whether or not on the same floor)—*

*(a) which forms part of a building;*

*(b) either the whole or a material part of which lies above or below some other part of the building; and*

*(c) in which all three basic amenities are available for the exclusive use of its occupants.*

## Section 255, Housing Act 2004: HMO declarations

*(1)      If a local housing authority are satisfied that*

*subsection (2) applies to a building or part of a building in their area, they may serve a notice under this section (an "HMO declaration") declaring the building or part to be a house in multiple occupation.*

(2) *This subsection applies to a building or part of a building if the building or part meets any of the following tests (as it applies without the sole use condition)—*

    (a) *the standard test (see section 254(2)),*

    (b) *the self-contained flat test (see section 254(3)), or*

    (c) *the converted building test (see section 254(4)), and the occupation, by persons who do not form a single household, of the living accommodation or flat referred to in the test in question constitutes a significant use of that accommodation or flat.*

(3) *In subsection (2) "the sole use condition" means the condition contained in—*

(a) section 254(2) (d) (as it applies for the purposes of the standard test or the self-contained flat test), or

(b) section 254(4) (e), as the case may be.

(4) The notice must—

(a) state the date of the authority's decision to serve the notice,

(b) be served on each relevant person within the period of seven days beginning with the date of that decision,

(c) state the day on which it will come into force if no appeal is made under subsection (9) against the authority's decision, and

(d) set out the right to appeal against the decision under subsection (9) and the period within which an appeal may be made.

(5) The day stated in the notice under subsection (4) (c) must be not less than 28 days after the date of the authority's decision to serve the notice.

(6) If no appeal is made under subsection (9) before the end of that period of 28 days, the notice comes into force on the day stated in the notice.

(7) If such an appeal is made before the end of that period of 28 days, the notice does not come into force unless and until a decision is given on the appeal which confirms the notice and either—

   (a) the period within which an appeal to the [Upper Tribunal] may be brought expires without such an appeal having been brought, or
   (b) if an appeal to the [Upper Tribunal] is brought, a decision is given on the appeal which confirms the notice.

(8) For the purposes of subsection (7), the withdrawal of an appeal has the same effect as a decision which confirms the notice appealed against.

(9) Any relevant person may appeal to a residential property tribunal against a decision of the local housing authority to serve an HMO declaration.

The appeal must be made within the period of 28

*days beginning with the date of the authority's decision.*

(10) *Such an appeal—*

   (a) *is to be by way of a re-hearing, but*

   (b) *may be determined having regard to matters of which the authority were unaware.*

(11) *The tribunal may—*

   (a) *confirm or reverse the decision of the authority, and*

   (b) *if it reverses the decision, revoke the HMO declaration.*

(12) *In this section and section 256 "relevant person", in relation to an HMO declaration, means any person who, to the knowledge of the local housing authority, is—*

   (a) *a person having an estate or interest in the building or part of the building* concerned (but is not a tenant under a lease with an unexpired term of 3 years of less), or

(b) a person managing or having control of that building or part (and not falling within paragraph (a)).

## Section 257, Housing Act 2004: HMOs: certain converted blocks of flats

(1) For the purposes of this section a "converted block of flats" means a building or part of a building which—

(a) has been converted into, and

(b) consists of, self-contained flats.

(2) This section applies to a converted block of flats if—

(a) building work undertaken in connection with the conversion did not comply with the appropriate building standards and still does not comply with them; and

(b) less than two-thirds of the self-contained flats are owner-occupied.

(3) In subsection (2) "appropriate building standards" means—

(a) in the case of a converted block of flats—

(i) on which building work was completed before 1st June 1992 or which is dealt with by regulation 20 of the Building Regulations 1991 (S.I. 1991/2768), and

(ii) which would not have been exempt under those Regulations, building standards equivalent to those imposed, in relation to a building or part of a building to which those Regulations applied, by those Regulations as they had effect on 1st June 1992; and

(b) in the case of any other converted block of flats, the requirements imposed at the time in relation to it by regulations under *section 1 of the Building Act 1984 (c.55).*

(4) *For the purposes of subsection (2) a flat is "owner-occupied" if it is occupied—*

    (a) *by a person who has a lease of the flat which has been granted for a term of more than 21 years,*

    (b) *by a person who has the freehold estate in the converted block of flats, or*

    (c) *by a member of the household of a person within paragraph (a) or (b).*

(5) *The fact that this section applies to a converted block of flats (with the result that it is a house in multiple occupation under section 254(1) (e)), does not affect the status of any flat in the block as a house in multiple occupation.*

(6) *In this section "self-contained flat" has the same meaning as in section 254.*

## Section 258, Housing Act 2004: HMOs: persons not forming a single household

(1) *This section sets out when persons are to be*

*regarded as not forming a single household for the purposes of section 254.*

(2) *Persons are to be regarded as not forming a single household unless—*

(a) *they are all members of the same family,* or

(b) *their circumstances are circumstances of a description specified for the purposes of this section in regulations made by the appropriate national authority.*

(3) *For the purposes of subsection (2) (a) a person is a member of the same family as another person if—*

(a) *those persons are married to each other or live together as husband and wife (or in an equivalent relationship in the case of persons of the same sex);*

(b) *one of them is a relative of the other; or*

(c) *one of them is, or is a relative of, one member of a couple and the other is a relative of the other member of the couple.*

(4)  For those purposes—

   (a)  *a "couple" means two persons who are married to each other or otherwise fall within subsection (3)(a);*

   (b)  *"relative" means parent, grandparent, child, grandchild, brother, sister, uncle, aunt, nephew, niece or cousin; a relationship of the half-blood shall be treated as a relationship of the whole blood; and*

   (d)  *the stepchild of a person shall be treated as his child.*

(5)  *Regulations under subsection (2)(b) may, in particular, secure that a group of persons are to be regarded as forming a single household only where (as the regulations may require) each member of the group has a prescribed relationship, or at least one of a number of prescribed relationships, to any one or more of*

*the others.*

*(6) In subsection (5) "prescribed relationship" means any relationship of a description specified in the regulations.*

## Section 259, HMOs: persons treated as occupying premises as only or main residence

*(1) This section sets out when persons are to be treated for the purposes of section 254 as occupying a building or part of a building as their only or main residence.*

*(2) A person is to be treated as so occupying a building or part of a building if it is occupied by the person—*

*(a) As the person's residence for the purpose of undertaking a full-time course of further or higher education;*

*(b) as a refuge, or*

*(c) In any other circumstances which are circumstances of a description specified for the purposes of this section in*

> *regulations made by the appropriate national authority.*

(3) *In subsection (2) (b) "refuge" means a building or part of a building managed by a voluntary organisation and used wholly or mainly for the temporary accommodation of persons who have left their homes as a result of—*

> *(a) physical violence or mental abuse, or*

> *(b) threats of such violence or abuse, from persons to whom they are or were married or with whom they are or were co-habiting.*

\**Section 256 Housing Act 2004* is not included as it is outside of the scope of this book.

## 5.2. Licensing of HMO's

The *Licensing of Houses in Multiple Occupation (Prescribed Description) (England) Order 2006* sets out the description of HMOs that are required to be licensed in all parts of England.

Under the Housing Act 2004 there are three types of licensing:

### 1. Compulsory licensing

Properties that meet the description below are subject to compulsory licensing.

- Three or more storeys high and
- Occupied by five or more persons and
- Those persons form two or more separate households

Compulsory licensing is governed by *Section 61 Housing Act 2004.*

### 2. Additional licensing of HMOs

Local Authorities have a discretionary power to apply additional licensing to a HMO in designated areas within their Borough. Additional licensing is governed by *Section 56-60 Housing Act 2004.*

## 3. Selective licensing of other residential accommodation

Properties that are subject to HMO licensing could be covered under a selective licensing scheme. A Local Authority may declare that certain areas, for example, where there is low demand for housing and/or high levels of anti-social behaviour, are appropriate for selective licensing. This licensing would cover all forms of private rented housing, including HMOs. Selective licensing is governed by *Section 79, 80 and 81 Housing Act 2004*.

## Additional criteria

The property must be registered with the Local Authority as a HMO and the Local Authority will provide a license to the HMO if it meets the following criteria:

- The HMO is reasonably suitable for occupation by the number of people allowed under the licence.
- The proposed licence holder is a fit, proper and

competent person.
- The proposed licence holder (or proposed manager, if there is one) is the most appropriate person to hold the licence.
- The proposed management and funding arrangements are satisfactory.

## **5.3. Requirements of a HMO**

A House in Multiple Occupation must meet the prescribed requirements set out in the checklist to ensure that it is fit for occupation:

## **Checklist**

- Satisfactory facilities for the storage, preparation and cooking of food.

- An (adequate) number of suitably located water closets for the exclusive use of the occupants.

- An (adequate) number of baths, showers and basins which each have a supply of hot and cold water.

- Fire escapes, fire alarms and other fire precautions.

## 5.4. Management regulations under the Housing Health and Safety Rating System (HHSRS)

All HMOs, whether the landlord needs a license or not, are subject to **Management Regulations** and **Inspections** under the **Housing Health and Safety Rating System (HHSRS) Housing Act 2004**.

This ensures that the property is managed properly and meets certain safety standards.

The landlord/manager must look after:
- The exterior of the dwelling and structural elements of the dwelling, and
- The inside facilities which are part of the dwelling.

The **Housing Health and Safety Rating System (*HHSRS*)** is a risk based evaluation tool to help Local Authorities identify and protect against potential risks and hazards to health and safety from any deficiencies identified in dwellings. It was introduced under the *Housing Act 2004* and came into effect on the 6th April 2006. It applies to residential properties in England.

The *HHSRS* assesses 29 categories of housing hazard and each hazard has a weighting which will help determine whether the property is rated as having Category 1 (Serious) hazards or Category 2 (Other) hazards.

The 29 categories of housing hazards can be found in the *Housing Health and Safety Rating System Operating Guidance- Annex D: Profiles of potential health and safety hazards in dwellings*. A copy of the guidance can be found using the link below:

http://www.communities.gov.uk/documents/housing/pdf/142631.pdf

## 5.5. Management of HMO (England) Regulations 2006

The Management Regulations place certain duties

upon owners or managers of HMOs which include:

- The duty of the manager to provide information to occupiers.

- The duty of the manager to take safety measures (including gas, electrical and fire safety).

- The duty of the manager to maintain water supply and drainage.

- The duty of the manager to supply and maintain gas and electricity.

- The duty of the manager to maintain common parts, fixtures, fitting and appliances.

- The duty of the manager to maintain living accommodation.

- The duty of the manager to provide waste disposal facilities.

- The duty of the manager to inform the Council about occupancy of the HMO.

The Regulations require that the specified standards of management are achieved and maintained. If a manager fails to meet those standards, the Local Authority may prosecute the manager which could result in maximum fines of £5,000 for breach of each Regulation.

The Regulations also impose duties on the occupiers of a HMO to ensure that the manager can comply with the Regulations. For example, occupiers are under a duty to comply with reasonable instructions about fire safety etc.

Full details of *The Management of Houses in Multiple Occupation (England) Regulations 2006 No. 372*, can be found at www.legislation.gov.uk

The Management Regulations and Inspections under the Housing Health and Safety Rating System (HHSRS) state that within the first five years of the Local Authority granting the HMO a licence the

Local Authority must ensure that there are no Part 1 functions that ought to be exercised by them in relation to premises in respect of which the licensing application is made.

## **Part 1 functions, Section 5 Housing Act 2004**

### *Category 1 hazards: general duty to take enforcement action*

(1)      *If a local housing authority considers that a category 1 hazard exists on any residential premises, they must take the appropriate enforcement action in relation to the hazard.*

(2)      *In subsection (1) "the appropriate enforcement action" means whichever of the following courses of action is indicated by subsection (3) or (4)—*

        (a)     *serving an improvement notice under section 11;*

        (b)     *making a prohibition order under section 20;*

        (c)     *serving a hazard awareness notice under section 28;*

(d)    taking emergency remedial action under section 40;

(e)    making an emergency prohibition order under section 43;

(f)    making a demolition order under subsection (1) or (2) of section 265 of the Housing Act 1985 (c. 68);

(g)    declaring the area in which the premises concerned are situated to be a clearance area by virtue of section 289(2) of that Act.

(3)    If only one course of action within subsection (2) is available to the authority in relation to the hazard, they must take that course of action.

(4)    If two or more courses of action within subsection (2) are available to the authority in relation to the hazard, they must take the course of action which they consider to be the most appropriate of those available to them.

(5)    The taking by the authority of a course of action within subsection (2) does not prevent subsection (1) from requiring them to take in relation to the same hazard—

*(a) either the same course of action again or another such course of action, if they consider that the action taken by them so far has not proved satisfactory, or*

*(b) another such course of action, where the first course of action is that mentioned in subsection (2)(g) and their eventual decision under section 289(2F) of the Housing Act 1985 means that the premises concerned are not to be included in a clearance area.*

*(6) To determine whether a course of action mentioned in any of paragraphs (a) to (g) of subsection (2) is "available" to the authority in relation to the hazard, see the provision mentioned in that paragraph.*

*(7) Section 6 applies for the purposes of this section.*

## Duties of Landlords and Managers of HMOs.

*Section 234, Housing Act 2004:* Management Regulations in respect of HMOs sets out the duties that the landlord or manager must adhere to in the management of a HMO.

## Section 234, Housing Act 2004: Management regulations in respect of HMOs

*(1)  The appropriate national authority may by regulations make provision for the purpose of ensuring that, in respect of every house in multiple occupation of a description specified in the regulations—*

   *(a)  there are in place satisfactory management arrangements; and*

   *(b)  satisfactory standards of management are observed.*

*(2)  The regulations may, in particular—*

   *(a)  impose duties on the person managing a house in respect of the repair, maintenance, cleanliness and good order of the house and facilities and equipment in it;*

   *(b)  impose duties on persons occupying a house for the purpose of ensuring that the person managing the house can effectively carry out any duty imposed on*

*him by the regulations.*

*(3) A person commits an offence if he fails to comply with a regulation under this section.*

*(4) In proceedings against a person for an offence under subsection (3) it is a defence that he had a reasonable excuse for not complying with the regulation.*

*(5) A person who commits an offence under subsection (3) is liable on summary conviction to a fine not exceeding level 5 on the standard scale.*

## Summary

If the landlord or manager fails to manage the property and observe the statutory management requirements the tenant should report any breach of the statutory requirements to the Local Authority who will investigate the matter and take appropriate action.

## 5.6. Inspection of a HMO by the Local Authority

The inspection of a HMO by the Local Authority will encompass an examination of all the parts and areas of the property. In the shared areas, the assessment of the property must look at any increase in the likelihood and/or outcomes of hazards arising which could arise because of the sharing of the property.

## 5.7. Enforcement Action by the Local Authority

A Local Authority has the power to take the following courses of enforcement action against a landlord or managing agent who is in breach of their duty as a manager of a HMO:

### Serve an Improvement Notice

An Improvement Notice is a notice requiring the person on whom it is served to take such remedial action in respect of the hazard concerned. Improvement notices are governed by *Section 11-19, Housing Act 2004*.

### Make a Prohibition Order

A Prohibition Order may prohibit the use of part or all the premises for some or all purposes or occupation by numbers or description of people. Prohibition Orders are governed by *Section 20-27, Housing Act 2004.*

### Serve a Hazard Awareness Notice

A hazard awareness notice may be served for a less serious hazard, where the Local Authority wants to draw attention to the desirability of remedial action. Hazard Awareness Notices are governed by *Section 28-29, Housing Act 2004.*

### Emergency measures

Local Authorities have a discretion to take emergency enforcement action against hazards which present an imminent risk of serious harm to occupiers. The Local Authority will either take remedial action to remove a hazard and recover reasonable expenses, or they will prohibit the use of part or all the property. Emergency measures are governed by *Section 40-45, Housing Act 2004.*

## Demolition orders

If a property is unfit to live in, the Local Authority may serve a Demolition Order. This requires the owners to demolish the property at their own expense, but they keep the land for their own use. A Demolition Order is only used when a house is beyond repair and can be knocked down without affecting other properties. Demolition Orders are governed by *Section 46, Housing Act 2004.*

## Clearance

A Local Authority can declare an area a clearance area if it is satisfied that each of the residential buildings in the area contains one or more Category 1 hazards (or that these buildings are dangerous or harmful to the health or safety of the inhabitants because of their bad arrangement or the narrowness or bad arrangement of the street) or any other buildings in the area are dangerous or harmful to the health of the inhabitants. Slum clearance is governed by *Section 47, Housing Act 2004*.

## 5.8. Disrepair in a HMO

The landlord and or/manager of a HMO has additional statutory duties to address disrepair and health and safety issues within the HMO. These duties are defined by *The Management of Houses in Multiple Occupation (England) Regulations 2006 No. 372*.

The duties apply to both landlord/manager and residents of HMO's and either could be prosecuted if found in breach of duty to maintain the dwelling in good and safe working order.

If the HMO is in a state of disrepair a Local Authority may serve a notice on the landlord/manager requiring the execution of works. If the landlord/manager fails to complete the works, the Local Authority may commence works and recharge the landlord/managing agent for the cost of completing the works.

## 5.9. Penalties for failing to licence a HMO

It is an offence for the landlord/manager in control of the property:

- To fail to apply for a licence for a licensable property; or
- To allow a property to be occupied by more people than are permitted under the licence.

## Financial penalties

A landlord/manager operating an unlicensed HMO faces a fine of up to £20,000 and a criminal record.

A landlord or person acting on his behalf who breaks any of the licence conditions faces fines of up to £5,000 for each breach.

## Non- financial penalties

If the property is a HMO subject to mandatory licensing and it is not registered as a HMO the landlord will be prohibited from serving a Section 21 Notice of seeking possession.

A licence will not be granted if the property is:

- Not suitable for the number of occupants.
- Not properly managed.
- Or the landlord or manager is not a fit and proper person.

**Rent Repayment Orders**

A tenant living in an unlicensed HMO can make an application to the First-Tier Tribunal Property Chamber (Residential Property) to claim back any rent they have paid to the landlord during the unlicensed period (up to a maximum of twelve months) *.

The First -Tier Tribunal Property Chamber (Residential Property) is the umbrella organisation for the five regional offices called Rent Assessment Panels, which provide an independent service in England for settling disputes involving private rented and leasehold property.

Further information can be found at the website: www.justice.gov.uk/tribunals/residential-property

The right of recovery is only available against a landlord who received rent from the tenants of the property.

*The First-Tier Tribunal will only make a Rent Repayment Order to the tenant if the landlord has been (criminally) convicted of operating an unlicensed HMO or the Local Authority has made a successful application to the Magistrates Court in respect of housing benefit. The statutory provision is set out below:

**Section 73, Housing Act 2004; other consequences of operating unlicensed HMOs: Rent Repayment orders:**

*S73 (8) If the application is made by an occupier of a part of the HMO, the tribunal must be satisfied as to the following matters—*

> *(a) that the appropriate person has been convicted of an offence under section 72(1) in relation to the HMO, or has been*

required by a rent repayment order to make a payment in respect of housing benefit paid in connection with occupation of a part or parts of the HMO,

(b) that the occupier paid, to a person having control of or managing the HMO, periodical payments in respect of occupation of part of the HMO during any period during which it appears to the tribunal that such an offence was being committed in relation to the HMO, and

(d) that the application is made within the period of 12 months beginning with—

(i) the date of the conviction or order,

or

(ii) if such a conviction was followed by such an order (or vice versa), the date of the later of them.

A tenant can apply for a Rent Repayment Order on application form: **FORM RR02: Application by occupier for a rent repayment order**. The

application form can be downloaded from the RPT website at:
www.rpts.gov.uk/pubs_and_forms/publications.htm
or telephone: 0845 600 3178 to request a form.

The tenant will be required to attach the following documents to their application:

a) Evidence of the successful prosecution or RRO for housing benefits provided by the Local Authority.

b) Evidence of the rent paid during the period of up to twelve months. If the landlord did not give the tenant a rent book or receipts for the rent the tenant is advised to make a list of the rent payments made and who they were paid to.

c) If the tenant and/or any other tenants in the house have appointed someone to represent them include all the agreements to appoint that person to act on their behalf.

d) Evidence of five or more tenants living in the house during the period of the claim, unless stated in (b) above.

Unfortunately, if the Local Authority fails to act against the landlord, the tenant will not be able to pursue an application for a rent repayment order. Further information on the procedure can be found at the www.justice.gov.uk website.

## 5.10. STEP BY STEP GUIDE

A tenant should follow the Step by Step Guide if they believe that they are occupying a HMO and they are not satisfied with any aspect of the condition and management of the HMO.

1. Check if the property falls within the definition of a House in Multiple Occupation (HMO).

2. If the property is a HMO, the tenant should contact the Local Authority to find out if the property is subject to mandatory (or additional/selective licensing) and does the property have a HMO license?

3. If the property is a licensed HMO and the landlord/managing agent has failed to carry out repair works to the building, the tenant can request that the Local Authority inspect the property using the powers contained in the Housing Act 2004.

4. If the property meets the definition of a HMO

and it is unlicensed the landlord will be liable for a fine.

5. If the HMO property is subject to disrepair the tenant should follow the step by step guide at the end of Chapter 4.

# CHAPTER SIX

# Possession Proceedings

This chapter applies to Rent Act, Secure, Assured and Assured Shorthold tenants.

This Chapter will set out what steps the landlord must take to obtain lawful possession of the property. If the landlord does not follow the correct legal procedure and attempts to evict a tenant unlawfully, the tenant should refer to the Step by Step Guide at the end of Chapter 3.

If a tenancy type is not listed here the tenant should contact Shelter or their local Citizens Advice Bureau for further advice and assistance.

**A useful starting point!**

The correct procedure to end a tenancy will depend on whether the tenancy is within the fixed term or periodic term.

## Definition: Fixed Term Tenancies

A fixed term tenancy is a tenancy for a definite period during which time the tenant and the landlord are bound by the terms of the agreement. Fixed term tenancies are governed by the terms of the tenancy agreement.

During the fixed term period, the landlord can only commence possession proceedings if the tenant breaches one of the grounds for possession. A landlord cannot obtain possession against a Rent Act tenant during the fixed term of the tenancy.

## Periodic Tenancies

Once the fixed term period of a tenancy expires the tenancy becomes a periodic tenancy. A periodic tenancy automatically follows the fixed-term if the parties do nothing (i.e. they do not sign another agreement). The tenancy will continue with the same terms as the fixed term tenancy. The period of the tenancy is determined by the frequency of the payment schedule.

- If the rent was paid monthly under the original fixed term tenancy, the tenancy will become a monthly periodic tenancy.

- If the rent was paid quarterly (every three months) the tenancy will be a quarterly tenancy.

- If the rent is paid annually the tenancy will be a six-month periodic tenancy.

## 6.1. Rent Act Tenancy

A Rent Act tenancy is governed by the Rent Act 1977. The Rent Act 1977 created two types of tenancy, a **'Protected tenancy'** and a **'Statutory tenancy'** which are referred to as **'Regulated tenancies'**.

## Definition of a Rent Act Tenancy:

The definition of a Rent Act tenancy is set out in *Section 1, Rent Act 1977* as a tenancy under which a dwelling- house (which may be a house or part of a house) is let as a separate dwelling.

## Protected Tenancy

A protected tenancy is a contractual tenancy and will come to an end in accordance with the terms in the tenancy agreement.

## Statutory Tenancy

If a protected tenant remains in occupation of the property upon expiration of the contractual term the tenancy will become a statutory tenancy. The statutory tenancy will continue on the same terms and conditions as the contractual tenancy. *Section 2(1) (a), Rent Act 1977.*

## Features of a Rent Act Tenancy:

A Rent Act tenancy has the following features:

- A Rent Act tenant has the right to a 'fair rent'. Fair rents are a form of rent control applicable for most self-contained private sector rented accommodation which was let before 15 January 1989. The Rent Act 1977 provides the rules for setting Fair Rents and the Rent Acts (Maximum Fair Rent) Order 1999 limits the amount of rent that can be charged by linking increases to the Retail Prices Index.

- If the landlord wants to increase the rent they must apply to the Rent Officer for a rent to be registered one year and nine months after the effective date of the last registration, however the new registered rent will not become effective until the two-year period has elapsed.

- The rent cannot be increased during the protected period of the tenancy.

- The landlord is required to serve a Notice of Increase in the prescribed form on the tenant if they want to increase the rent. *Section 49, Rent Act 1977.*This notice of increase will provide details of the new rent and the date that it is effective from. If the tenant is in receipt of housing benefit they should take this form to their local housing benefit office. A tenant will not be liable for the new rent until they receive the Notice of Increase from the landlord.

- A Rent Act tenancy is granted for an initial fixed term period (**Protected tenancy**). Once the fixed term ends/or the landlord serves a valid 'Notice to Quit', or a "Notice of Rent Increase" the tenancy becomes a (**Statutory tenancy**). A statutory tenancy means that the tenant has rights governed by statute to pay rent and continue in occupation under rent control or other legislation.

- The landlord can only apply for possession once the tenancy becomes a statutory tenancy.

- Possession can only be applied for on the Grounds (called Cases) contained with *Schedule 15 of the Rent Act 1977*. The Grounds (Cases) are divided into Mandatory and Discretionary grounds.

## Definition: Mandatory and Discretionary Grounds

The grounds for possession of property falls into two categories:

## Mandatory Grounds:

The Court must order that the tenant give up possession of the property if the landlord can prove that the tenant has breached the terms of the tenancy.

## Discretionary Grounds:

The Court can use its discretion based on all the facts to decide whether an order for possession should be made.

## Termination of a Rent Act Tenancy by a tenant

## Protected Tenancy

A tenant must end a protected tenancy in accordance with the terms stated in the tenancy agreement.

### Statutory Tenancy

The tenant must serve the landlord with a Notice to Quit in writing if s/he wishes to give up possession of the property. The notice period will be the period stated in the protected tenancy agreement. If no notice period is stated, the notice period is three months.

### Termination of a Rent Act Tenancy by the Landlord

### Protected Tenancy

The landlord can only end the tenancy during the contractual period in accordance with the terms stated in the tenancy agreement.

The tenancy can be terminated in the following ways:

- Expiration of the fixed term tenancy.
- Notice to Quit served by the Landlord.

- Surrender (operation of the law or express agreement).
- Service of a notice of increase of rent.

**Statutory Tenancy**

The landlord will only be entitled to possession once the contractual tenancy has come to an end. The landlord can then end the tenancy by serving a Notice to Quit on the tenant.

The landlord must issue a claim for possession at Court and at the hearing satisfy the Court that one of the Grounds (Cases) of the tenancy has been breached by the tenant and thus they are entitled to possession.

**6.2. Secure Tenancy**

A Secure tenancy is governed by the *Housing Act 1985*. Secure tenancies are tenancies which are granted by a public body to an individual who occupies the dwelling as his/her only or principal home.

## Definition of Secure Tenancies:

A Secure tenancy is defined in *Section 79(1), Housing Act 1985* which states:

*A tenancy under which a dwelling house (house or part of a house) is let as a separate dwelling is a secure tenancy if the conditions described in Sections 80 and 81(the landlord and tenant condition) are satisfied.*

## The Landlord Condition: Section 80 Housing Act 1985

Landlords that can offer secure tenancies:
- A Local Authority
- Development Corporation
- A Housing Action Trust
- An Urban Development Corporation

## The Tenant Condition: Section 81 Housing Act 1985

The definition of a tenant condition is that the tenant is an individual and occupies the dwelling-house as his only or principal home; or, where the tenancy is a joint tenancy, that each of the joint tenants is an individual and at least one of them occupies the dwelling-house as his only or principal home.

## Features of a Secure Tenancy

A Secure tenancy has the following features:

- Secure tenancies are not subject to any restrictions on what rent can be charged.

- The landlord must serve the tenant with a Section 8 Notice of Seeking Possession which meets the requirements of *Section 83 Housing Act 1985* if they intend to make an application to Court for possession of the property.

- Proceedings for possession of property must be issued within 12 months from the date of service of a Section 8 Notice of Seeking Possession on the tenant.

- To gain possession of a secure tenancy, the landlord must prove one or more of the statutory grounds of possession set out in *Schedule 2, Housing Act 1985*.

- The Grounds of Possession for Secure tenancies as contained in Schedule 2, Housing Act 1985 are all discretionary grounds.

- The tenant can terminate the tenancy by surrendering the tenancy by agreement or by serving a Notice to Quit on the landlord.

## Termination of a Secure Tenancy by the Tenant

The tenant can bring the tenancy to an end by:

- Serving a Notice to Quit on the landlord

- Serving a Notice of Surrender on the landlord.

## Termination of a Secure Tenancy by the Landlord

A Secure tenancy can only be ended by the landlord once they have served the appropriate notice(s) (as below) and obtained a Court Order for possession.

- Notice to Quit.

- Section 8 Notice of Seeking Possession. (The requirements of a Section 8 Notice of Seeking Possession are set out at Section 6.7.)

- Obtaining a demotion order under *Section 82A Housing Act 1985*. (Demotion Order: A demoted tenancy is a tenancy issued by order of a Court. It lasts for one year, unless it is extended in which case it would last for eighteen months. The secure tenancy will be then replaced with a less secure 'demoted' tenancy, by a Demotion Order from the Court.)

## 6.3. Assured Tenancy

An Assured tenancy is governed by the *Housing Act 1988*. Assured tenancies are granted by Registered Social Landlords (RSLs) also known as Housing Associations.

## Definition of Assured Tenancies

The definition of an assured tenancy is contained within *Section 1, Housing Act 1988* which is summarised as follows:

*A tenancy of a dwelling house let to an individual who occupies the property as his or her only or principal home.*

## Features of an Assured tenancy:

An assured tenancy has the following features;

- The landlord seeking possession must serve a Section 8 Notice of Seeking Possession on the tenant before they commence possession proceeding in the local County Court.

- The landlord can obtain possession on the Grounds which are contained in *Schedule 2 Housing Act 1988*.

- The Grounds for possession are mandatory and discretionary.

## **6.4. Assured Shorthold Tenancy**

All tenancies which are created after the 28th February 1997 by a private landlord are automatically Assured Shorthold tenancies. However, if a tenancy comes within the following exceptions it will not be classified as an Assured Shorthold tenancy.

The exceptions are set out in *Schedule 2A Housing Act 1988* and can be summarised as follows:

- If the landlord serves the tenant with a notice that the tenancy is not an assured shorthold tenancy.

- The tenancy agreement states that the tenancy is not an assured short hold tenancy.

- An assured tenancy was previously a secure tenancy.

- An assured tenancy which was granted following a succession of a Rent Act tenancy.

- A tenancy created after 28 February 1997 which replaced an assured tenancy will not be an assured short hold tenancy unless the landlord serves a notice on the landlord stating that the tenancy will be an assured shorthold tenancy.

- Assured agricultural occupancies.

- An assured tenancy arising by *Schedule 10 to the Local Government and Housing Act 1989* (security of tenure on ending of long residential tenancies).

This section only provides information on the legal procedure that must be followed to obtain possession of an assured shorthold tenancy which does not fall within any of the exceptions.

If a tenancy falls within the exceptions listed above the tenancy will not be an assured shorthold tenancy and the tenant should contact a Solicitor to obtain further advice about their rights.

## **Features of an Assured Shorthold tenancy**

An Assured short hold tenancy has the following features:

- The house or flat is let as separate accommodation and is the tenant's main home.

- The landlord cannot usually claim possession during the first six months of the tenancy.

- The landlord cannot claim possession during the fixed term of the tenancy unless the tenant breaches any of the grounds for possession contained in *Schedule 2, Housing Act 1988*.

- The landlord can apply for possession using the mandatory ground for possession under Section 21 Housing Act 1988 after the fixed term of the tenancy has ended.

- If the tenant remains in occupation after the

fixed term period, the tenant will become a statutory periodic tenant pursuant to *Section 5 (2) of the Housing Act 1988.*

### 6.5. Fixed Term Tenancies

Schedule 7 Housing and Planning Act 2016 makes amendments to the Housing Acts 1985 and 1996 so that, from the commencement of Part 4 of the Housing and Planning Act 2016, Local Authorities will be required to grant new tenants a fixed-term tenancy, either secure or introductory, for a period of between 2 and 10 years (if the tenant has a child under 9 years old then the fixed term tenancy must be granted for a period until the child turns 19 years old)

These fixed term tenants will have the same rights as a secure (introductory) tenant for the duration of the fixed term.

If the tenancy is not renewed beyond the fixed term period, the landlord must commence possession proceedings before the period of 3 months beginning with the day on which the tenancy ended. A court must make a possession order if they are satisfied that:

- The landlord has complied with all of the requirements of sections 86A to 86C, Housing Act 1985,
- the tenancy that was the subject of the review section 86A, Housing Act 1985 has ended,
- the proceedings were commenced before the end of the period of 3 months beginning with the day on which the tenancy ended, and
- the only fixed term tenancy still in existence is a new secure tenancy arising by virtue of section 86D, Housing Act 1985.

But the court may refuse to grant an order for possession under this section if the court considers that a decision of the landlord under section 86A or 86C was wrong in law.

### 6.6. Notices (to end the Tenancy)

It is a legal requirement that a landlord must serve a valid notice on the tenant to recover possession of the tenanted property. The service of a notice is the first step in commencing possession proceedings.

**6.7. Section 8 Notice of Seeking Possession**

A landlord will serve a Section 8 Notice of Seeking Possession if the tenant has breached a term of the tenancy agreement.

A Section 8 Notice of Seeking Possession is governed by *Section 8 Housing Act 1988* as amended by the Housing Act 1996. A Section 8 Notice of Seeking Possession can be served on a tenant who has a Secure, Assured and Assured Shorthold tenancy. A Section 8 Notice of Seeking Possession must:

- Be in the Prescribed Form 3 (SI 2016 No.1118); This form is to be used for Assured, Assured Agricultural and Assured Shorthold tenancies

- Specify the Ground(s) on which the Landlord is seeking possession;

- Lay out the Particulars of the Ground(s) for possession.

- State the date after which proceedings may be commenced.

- State that, proceedings will not begin later than 12 months from the date of service of the notice.

## What should a tenant do if they are served with a Section 8 Notice of Seeking Possession?

A Section 8 Notice of Seeking Possession must specify a date by which the tenant should remedy the breach. If the tenant fails to remedy the breach by the specified date, only then can the landlord commence Court proceedings to obtain possession of the property. Upon receipt of the Section 8 Notice of Seeking Possession, the tenant should contact the landlord and attempt to reach an agreement to prevent the landlord taking further action.

An example of a Section 8 Notice of Seeking Possession can be found at Annex 2.

## Section 21 Notice Requiring Possession

A Section 21 Notice Requiring Possession is used for no-fault ground possessions. If the tenant has breached a term of the tenancy agreement the landlord cannot serve a Section 21 Notice Requiring Possession to claim possession.

### 6.8. Notice to Quit (NTQ)

A Notice to Quit is a notice, required by law, enabling the tenant or landlord to terminate a periodic tenancy and gain possession of the property.

A Notice to Quit is governed by common law and is only enforceable against someone who has basic occupation rights, e.g. is a trespasser, a tenant who has a resident landlord or if the tenant is failing to occupy their Secure/Assured tenancy as their only and principal home.

## Definition: Resident Landlords

A resident landlord lives in the same building or property as the tenant. If the property is split into purpose built flats with the landlord and tenant in different flats, or the landlord does not live in the same property as the tenant then it is not a resident landlord letting.

If the tenant receives a Notice to Quit from their landlord, they should check that it is valid by using the checklist below. The Notice must be:

- In writing and contain prescribed information. (Prescribed information means information required by law.)

- The Notice to Quit must be for the correct length of time. The length of the Notice to Quit must correspond to the period of the tenancy e.g. if the tenancy is a monthly tenancy then the notice must not expire any earlier than one month from the date of its service. The exception to this rule is that a yearly tenancy only requires a six-month notice and the parties can agree to a lessor or greater notice period.

- The Notice to Quit must expire on the correct day. The correct day is either at the end of the current *period,* or on the first day of the subsequent period; the 'period' is the length of the periodic tenancy e.g. weekly, monthly, quarterly, six monthly and yearly etc.

- Service (delivery of the notice to the tenant) must be done in accordance with the terms of the tenancy agreement. The Notice to Quit should be served on the tenant or (joint) tenants.

- The notice should be served on or before the date from which the notice period begins to run.

- A Claim for Possession cannot be issued at Court until the Notice to Quit has expired.

An example of a Notice to Quit can be found at Annex 3.

## 6.9. Section 21 Notice Requiring Possession

A Section 21 notice can only be served on an Assured Shorthold tenant. It cannot be served on a Rent Act, Secure or Assured tenant.

A Section 21 Notice is governed by *Section 21, Housing Act 1988*.

## Requirements of a Section 21 Notice
## Assured Shorthold tenancies pre-1st October 2015

The Section 21 Notice requirements for tenancies that commenced before 1st October 2015 are set out below:

- A Section 21 Notice must not give the tenant less than two months' notice that the landlord requires possession of the dwelling house.

- A Section 21 Notice cannot expire during the fixed term of the tenancy.

- A Section 21 (1) (b) or (4) (a) notice contains no

time limit, therefore once the two months have expired, provided the notice has not been withdrawn or a new tenancy agreement signed, the landlord can issue a Claim for Possession of the property.

## Requirements of a Section 21 Notice post 1st October 2015

The new rules regarding Section 21 notices introduced by the Deregulation Act 2015 applies to new assured shorthold tenancies (ASTs) entered on or after 1st October 2015 in England & Wales. The new rules will apply to all tenancies from 1st October 2018. The new rules make the following changes to the Section 21 requirements:

- The landlord must use the prescribed Form 6A (The Assured Shorthold Tenancy Notices and Prescribed Requirements (England) (Amendment) Regulations 2015)

- A Section 21 (4) (a) Notice does not have to end on the last day of the period of the tenancy. *Section 35, Deregulation Act 2015.*

- The landlord cannot serve a tenant with a Section 21 notice within the first four months of the tenancy and if the tenancy is a replacement tenancy, the landlord cannot serve a Section 21 notice within the first four months of the original tenancy. * *Section 36, Deregulation Act 2015.*

*\*If the tenancy was originally a fixed term tenancy which became a statutory periodic tenancy at the end of the fixed term the above time limits do not apply.*

- Once a Section 21 notice is served the landlord must commence possession proceedings within six months. If the landlord fails to commence possession proceedings within six months, the Section 21 Notice will be invalid and the landlord will be required to serve a new Section 21 Notice. *Section 36, Deregulation Act 2015.*

- If the tenancy is a statutory periodic tenancy, then the landlord must commence court proceedings within four months of service of the Section 21 notice. *Section 36, Deregulation Act 2015.*

- A tenant of an assured shorthold tenancy will be entitled to a repayment of rent if the landlord has served a Section 21 Notice that has brought the tenancy to an end before the end of a period of a tenancy **and** the tenant had paid rent in advance for that period **and** the tenant was not in occupation of the property for one or more whole days of that period. If the repayment of rent has not been made when the court makes an order for possession under Section 21, the court must order the landlord to repay the amount of rent to which the tenant is entitled. *Section 40, Deregulation Act 2015.*

- A notice under Section 21 may not be permitted to be given by the landlord to the tenant if the landlord has failed to comply with prescribed requirements that may be imposed on a landlord. The *regulations prescribing certain requirements may relate to matters such as health and safety, property condition or energy performance certificates. *Section 38, Deregulation Act 2015.*

- The Secretary of State may by regulations require the landlord to give the tenant information about the rights and responsibilities of the landlord (or a person acting on behalf of such a landlord) and the tenant under an assured shorthold tenancy of a dwelling-house in England. A landlord will not be permitted to serve a Section 21 notice on a tenant if the landlord is in breach of the requirement in the regulations. *Section 39, Deregulation Act 2015.*

- A Section 21 Notice can also be served in accordance with a break clause in the tenancy agreement.

**Definition: Break Clause**

A break clause is a provision in a tenancy agreement which enables either the landlord or the tenant, or both, to end the tenancy early.

An example of a Section 21 Notice can be found at Annex 4.

**6.10. When will a Section 21 Notice be invalid?**

A Section 21 Notice will be invalid if either the notice has been completed incorrectly which would give the tenant a **Technical Defence** to the landlord's claim for possession.

And/or in the alternative the facts of the case invalidate the notice. This is a **Substantive Defence** to the landlord's claim for possession.

**Technical Defences**

- The landlord has issued possession proceedings in Court during the first four months of the tenancy.

- The landlord has served a Section 21 Notice and the landlord has issued possession proceedings in Court before the fixed term of the tenancy has ended.

- The Section 21 Notice does not provide the tenant with two calendar months 'written notice that the landlord requires possession of the property.

- The landlord has issued possession proceedings before the Section 21 notice has expired.

- The Section 21 Notice is not on the prescribed form.

**Substantive Defences**

- The property is a House in Multiple Occupation subject to mandatory or compulsory licensing and the landlord does not have a licence for the property. *Section 98 Housing Act 2004.*

- The landlord has failed to protect the tenant's tenancy deposit in one of the authorised tenancy deposit schemes and comply with the initial requirements of the scheme. *Section 212-215 Housing Act 2004.*

- The landlord has not provided the tenant with the full prescribed information.

- The tenant has complained about the condition of the property and that complaint has been upheld by the local authority by the service of an enforcement notice;

A tenant is advised to obtain legal advice to check if a Section 21 Notice is valid.

## 6.11. Revenge Evictions

For tenancies that started after the 1st October 2015, *Section 33, Deregulation Act 2015* will apply. Section 33 states that if a tenant complains about disrepair to the landlord in writing and the landlord does not provide a response within 14 days or the response provided is inadequate and the landlord serves a Section 21 Notice following the complaint, the Section 21 Notice will be invalid.

If the tenant then complains to the Local Authority about poor or unsafe property conditions and the Local Authority serves a * **relevant notice** on the landlord, the landlord will be prevented from evicting tenants by service of a Section 21 Notice for six months from the date that the relevant notice is served on the landlord.

If, however, the Local Authority inspect the property and decide that the issues complained of do not meet the criteria for service of a relevant notice then the landlord will be permitted to serve a Section 21 Notice on the tenant.

A relevant notice is defined as an **Improvement Notice** served under *Section 11 or Section 12 of the Housing Act 2004*, or a **Notice of Emergency Remedial Action** served under *Section 40(7), Housing Act 2004*.

An Improvement Notice is a notice requiring the landlord to take remedial action in respect of the hazard complained of.

A Notice of Emergency Remedial Action is a notice that requires the landlord to take such remedial action in respect of the hazard concerned as the Local Authority consider immediately necessary to remove the imminent risk of serious harm.

Section 33, Deregulation Act 2015 will not apply if the damage to the property has been caused by the tenant breaching their duty to treat the property in a tenant like manner or breaching an express term of the tenancy. Additionally, the section will not apply if at the time the Section 21 Notice is served the property is genuinely on the market for sale.

### 6.12. Accelerated Possession Procedure

The Accelerated Possession Procedure is the procedure used by landlords to claim possession of residential property. The procedure does not require a Court hearing and is only applicable to claims brought following service of a Section 21 Notice.

The landlord cannot use the Accelerated Possession Procedure if they are claiming that the tenant has breached one of the grounds for possession.

A landlord can use the Accelerated Possession Procedure to obtain possession if the case meets the requirements in Part 55.12 of the Civil

Procedure Rules.

## Civil Procedure Rules

The Civil Procedure Rules (CPR) are the rules of Civil Procedure used by the Court of Appeal, High Court of Justice and County Courts in civil cases in England and Wales.

The Civil Procedure Rules (CPR) can be found at: www.justice.gov.uk

## The requirements of CPR 55.12:

- An assured short hold tenancy was granted after the 15th January 1989.

- The only purpose is to recover possession of the property.

- The tenancy did not automatically follow an Assured Tenancy which was not an Assured short hold tenancy.

- The tenancy is subject to a written agreement or follows a tenancy that was a written tenancy.

- A Section 21 Notice has been served.

If the landlord uses the Accelerated Possession Procedure the tenant will receive a copy of the Claim form and a Response pack from the local County Court. The tenant has 14 days to file a Defence at Court. If the tenant files a Defence the Judge will decide whether the case should be listed for a hearing. If the Judge can find no discernable Defence then an Order for possession will be made without a Court hearing.

**6.13. Which Court?**

A Claim for Possession of property must be started in the County Court which is local to the property that the tenant occupies.

Tenants can search for their local County Court using the link below:

https://courttribunalfinder.service.gov.uk

## 6.14. Pre- Action Protocol for Possession Claims by Social Landlords

A social landlord (e.g. a local authority, registered social landlords, Housing Action Trust and private registered providers of social housing) is required to follow the **"Pre-Action Protocol for Possession Claims by Social Landlords"** when bringing a claim for possession based on rent arrears.

The protocol contains guidance on what steps the landlord is required to take to assist the tenant before commencing possession proceedings to recover rent arrears. The Court will consider whether the protocol has been followed when deciding what order to make.

If the landlord has unreasonably failed to comply with the terms of the protocol the court may impose one or more of the following sanctions—

(a) an order for costs; and

(b) in cases other than those brought solely on mandatory grounds, adjourn, strike out or dismiss claims. Paragraph 2.13 of the Pre-Action Protocol for Possession Claims by Social Landlords.

The "Pre-Action Protocol for Possession Claims by Social Landlords" can be found at the following link: www.justice.gov.uk/courts/procedurerules/civil/protocol/prot_rent

**Note:** The Pre- Action Protocol for Possession Claims by Social Landlords does not apply to private landlords.

### 6.15. Standard Possession Procedure Claims

If the landlord is claiming possession based on any of the Grounds contained within the Rent Act 1977, Housing Act 1985 and the Housing Act 1988 the landlord must make a Claim for Possession using Claim Form: N5 and Particulars of Claim on Form N119.

The Court will send the tenant a copy of the Claim Form, Particulars of Claim and copies of any supporting documents. The Court will also send the tenant a Response Pack which will include an Acknowledgment of Service Form and a Defence Form.

If the tenant disputes any of the grounds for possession, they are required to complete the Defence form and file it at Court within 28 days.

**Acknowledgement of Service**

A tenant can file an Acknowledgment of Service if s/he requires more time to file a Defence. The deadline for filing an Acknowledgment of Service is 14 days after receipt of the Claim Form and Particulars of Claim.

**6.16. Defences to Possession Claims**

The most common claims for possession are brought on the grounds of rent arrears therefore we have set out the most common Defences for rent arrears possession claims: E.G.

- If the tenant has disrepair in the property, the tenant can defend the claim for possession by filing a counterclaim for disrepair to be set off against the claim for rent arrears.

- If the landlord has failed to comply with the tenancy deposit scheme rules the tenant can file a counterclaim for the statutory penalty to be offset against the rent arrears.

- If the tenant has proof that they have made payments to the rent that the landlord has failed to include in the rent arrears schedule.

- Whilst not a Defence but mitigation, the Court may agree to the possession proceedings being adjourned to give the tenant time to resolve any housing benefit issues.

If the landlord is claiming possession following service of a Section 21 Notice, the Defences that can be raised are set out in Section 6.9.

## 6.17. The Hearing

At the hearing, the Judge will have to be satisfied on the facts that the landlord is entitled to possession of the property.

If the landlord applies for possession using any of the <u>Mandatory grounds</u> for possession, or <u>possession under s21 Housing Act 1988,</u> the Judge will have no choice but to make an Outright Possession Order if the landlord proves that the tenant is in breach of the mandatory grounds for possession and/or the requirements of s21 Housing Act 1988 have been fulfilled by the landlord.

If the landlord has applied for possession using the <u>Discretionary grounds</u> for possession the Judge must be satisfied that the grounds for possession are made out and that it is reasonable to make a possession order.

## 6.18. Types of Court Orders

### Outright Possession Order

An Outright Possession Order entitles the landlord to vacant possession of the property. The Outright Possession order for possession will take effect either forthwith (straightaway) or within 14 or 28 days after the Court hearing.

### Suspended Possession Order

A Suspended Possession Order means that the tenant is permitted to remain in property on the condition that they stick to the terms of the Suspended Possession Order. E.g. If the landlord was claiming possession based on rent arrears, the Court may order a Suspended Possession Order on terms that the tenant is required to pay full rent plus an amount towards the arrears.

If the tenant does not stick to the terms of the Suspended Possession order the landlord can apply to the court for a warrant of eviction.

## Adjournment

The Judge can adjourn the possession hearing if s/he is not satisfied that s/he can make a final decision on the case i.e. if further evidence is required or a decision that will have a bearing on the case is pending. The Judge can adjourn the case indefinitely or for a specific period with a return date.

## Dismissal/ Strike Out

The Judge may dismiss the landlord's claim for possession if the Judge is not satisfied that the landlord is entitled to possession.

## 6.19. Money Judgment

If the Court makes an order for possession on the grounds of rent arrears, the Court will also order a money judgment against the tenant.

A money judgement is a court order that will require the tenant to repay the landlord the amount claimed in the Particulars of Claim.

## 6.20. Court Costs

In possession cases the following costs rule applies in respect of court costs:

- A landlord will be entitled to claim their fixed costs from the tenant if they are successful in obtaining a possession order.

- If a possession order is made by the Judge the tenant may be ordered to pay the landlord's legal costs of commencing possession proceedings.

The rule about fixed costs are set out in Civil Procedure Rules: CPR:45.

## 6.21. Extra time to remain in the property on the grounds of exceptional hardship

If the Judge makes an Outright Possession Order the tenant can make an application for extra time to remain in the property on the grounds of exceptional hardship.

The Judge can grant a tenant a maximum of 42 days (6 weeks) to remain in the property if the Judge is satisfied that the tenant would suffer exceptional hardship if they were to be evicted on an earlier date. The tenant can request an extension of time on the grounds of exceptional hardship on the Defence form contained within the response pack. The Judge will consider the tenant's application at the first hearing. If the tenant does not make the application at the first hearing the application must be made before the eviction date using application form N244. If the application is made after the first hearing the application will be listed for a further hearing for the Judge to consider the application.

<u>CPR Part 55.18: Possession Claims</u>

*Postponement of possession*
**55.18**
*(1)    Where the defendant seeks postponement of possession on the ground of exceptional hardship under section 89 of the Housing Act 1980, the judge may direct a hearing of that*

*issue.*

(2) *Where the judge directs a hearing under paragraph (1) (a) the hearing must be held before the date on which possession is to be given up; and (b) the judge will direct how many days' notice the parties must be given of that hearing.*

(3) *Where the judge is satisfied, on a hearing directed under paragraph (1), that exceptional hardship would be caused by requiring possession to be given up by the date in the order of possession, he may vary the date on which possession must be given up.*

### 6.22. After the Hearing

After the possession hearing the Court will send the tenant a copy of the possession order which sets out the order that the Judge made at the possession hearing.

The possession order will specify what order has

been made by the Judge, the date the tenant has been ordered to leave the property, whether a money judgment has been made and any order for costs.

**Important**

If the tenant does not leave the property on the date specified on the possession order, the landlord cannot remove the tenant from the property. The landlord will be required to apply for a warrant of eviction to lawfully evict the tenant once the date for possession has passed.

The tenant will remain liable for the rent of the property (classified as a charge for use and occupation) until the warrant of eviction is executed by a court bailiff.

**6.23. Challenging the Possession Order**

The tenant may challenge the possession order by making an application at Court to either set aside or vary the possession order in the following circumstances:

- The tenant did not attend the hearing due to ill health/ exceptional circumstances.

- The tenant was not notified of the hearing date.

- The tenant did not receive the Court papers.

- The tenant filed a late response to the Claim.

If any of the above circumstances apply the tenant can make an application to Court to set aside or vary the Possession Order under Part 55.19 Civil Procedure Rules.

## Application to set aside or vary an order for possession: CPR 55.19

An application to either set aside or vary a possession order is governed by CPR 55.19. The tenant will be required to make an application within 14 days of being served with the Court Order.

The Court may:

(a) On application by a party within 14 days of service of the order; or

(b) Of its own initiative, set aside or vary any order made under rule 55.17

If a tenant makes an application to vary or set aside a possession order they will be required to meet all the requirements of **CPR Rule 39.3(5)**. The tenant will be required to satisfy the following:

- Show good reason for not attending the trial.
- Have acted promptly since finding out about the Order.
- Have a reasonable prospect of succeeding at trial.

If the tenant's application to vary or set aside the possession order is successful, the possession order will either be varied to a lessor order or set aside, and the tenant put back in the position they would have been in had the possession order not been made. If the possession order is set aside the Court will then list a new hearing date so that the case can be decided anew.

## 6.24. Warrant of Eviction

If the landlord has obtained an Outright Order for possession, or if the tenant has breached the terms of a Suspended Possession Order, the landlord will be entitled to make an application for a warrant of eviction once the date for possession on the possession order has expired.

Once a warrant of eviction application has been filed at Court, the Court will send the tenant a warrant of eviction notice confirming the date and time that the court bailiff will attend the property to execute the warrant.

When the bailiffs attend the property, they have the right to remove anybody who is still in occupation of the property by use of reasonable force. The landlord will very often instruct a locksmith to attend at the same time to change the locks to the property so that the tenant is unable to re-enter once evicted.

The landlord is not permitted to take any steps to remove the tenant from the property until the bailiffs have been instructed to attend and evict the tenant further to a warrant of eviction.

The date the bailiffs attend the property is the last possible date that the tenant is permitted to remain in the property. If the tenant has not found any accommodation by this date they should attend their local authorities' homeless persons' unit and make a homeless application. The Local Authority will assess the application and determine if the tenant is eligible for advice and/or assistance.

**6.25. Fast Track Evictions**

The landlord can include in their Claim for Possession a request that the enforcement of the possession order be transferred to the High Court. Alternatively, the landlord can make a request at the possession hearing if the Judge makes an Outright order for possession to have the enforcement of the possession order transferred to the High Court. The Judge will use their discretion when deciding whether the case should be transferred to the High Court. The landlord will most commonly advance

the following arguments to convince the Judge that the enforcement should be transferred,
namely delays using the County Court bailiffs, loss of rental income and risk of damage to the property amongst others which may be dependent upon the facts of the case.

If the landlord requests that enforcement be transferred to the High Court the tenant should challenge this at the possession hearing citing reasons why High court enforcement is not necessary, for example the lack of notice provided by High Court bailiffs especially if children, elderly or disabled persons are present in the property.

*Section 42(2) of the County Courts Act 1984* gives the county court a general power to transfer a case to the High Court and *Section 42(5)* provides that if proceedings for enforcement are transferred, the order may be enforced as a High Court order.

**Section 42 (2) & (5) County Courts Act 1984 Transfer to High Court by order of a county court.**

(2) Subject to any such provision, a county court may order the transfer of any proceedings before it to the High Court.

(5) Where proceedings for the enforcement of any judgment or order of a county court are transferred under this section–

> (a) the judgment or order may be enforced as if it were a judgment or order of the High Court; and
> 
> (b) subject to subsection (6), it shall be treated as a judgment or order of that court for all purposes.

Once the landlord has the sealed possession order from the Court they will be entitled to apply for permission (rule 3(2) of RSC Order 45) for a writ of possession/ writ of control (if recovering a money judgment) and have this sealed by the County Court in which the Possession Order was made.

Permission for a writ of possession will not be granted unless the Court is satisfied that the tenant had notice of the proceedings, (CPR 83.19) this does not mean notice of the application for permission to issue the writ. The application will then be sent to the High Court to be granted. Once the writ of possession/ (and if applicable the) writ of control has been granted the landlord can instruct a High Court enforcement officer to enforce the writ.

If the landlord applies for a combined writ of possession/control this will allow the High Court enforcement in addition to obtaining possession to also seize assets to set against any rent arrears and costs which are outstanding under the Possession Order.

Tenants should be advised that there is no requirement that they be notified of the application for permission to issue a writ of possession (rule 3(2) of RSC Order 45) and the date of the intended eviction once the landlord has been granted a writ of possession by the Court. The High Court bailiff will not send notice of the date that they are attending to enforce the writ to the landlord.

Rule 2(1) (d) of RSC Order 46 contains a further provision that the court's permission to issue a writ is necessary 'where under the judgment or order any person is entitled to a remedy subject to the fulfilment of any condition which it is alleged has been fulfilled'.

# CHAPTER SEVEN

# Housing Benefit

### 7.1. What is Housing Benefit?

Housing Benefit is available to help people on low incomes or who are in receipt of benefits with assistance towards paying their rent. Housing Benefit can pay an applicant's full rent or part of their rent depending on their financial circumstances.

A claim for housing benefit needs to be made at the local authorities' offices using a Housing benefit/Council tax benefit application form.

The rules for claiming Housing Benefit are numerous and complicated, therefore this Chapter aims to provide a general overview of the common requirements and rules for claiming Housing Benefit.

If a tenant claims Housing Benefit and they experience problems with their application, they are advised to contact their local Citizens Advice Bureau to obtain advice and assistance as it may be necessary to request a review or appeal the decision.

### 7.2. Eligibility for Housing Benefit

A tenant will be eligible for Housing Benefit if:

- They are liable to make payments in respect of a dwelling (property) which they occupy as their home.

- They are in receipt of a benefit which automatically entitles them to Housing benefit such as Income support, Income based JSA or ESA and Pension Credit.

- They are not a person from abroad.

- They pass the Right to Reside and Habitual residence test.

- They are not an excluded person.

- The arrangement is eligible for Housing Benefit (e.g. if renting from family members this arrangement may not be eligible for housing benefit).

Once the tenant makes a claim for housing benefit the Local Authority must process the application within 14 days or as soon as reasonably practical. The application may be delayed if the Local Authority requests further information to assess the tenant's claim. The tenant should supply the requested information within the stated deadline to prevent their claim being delayed. If a tenant is awarded Housing benefit it will only pay the eligible rent for the dwelling (property).

**Eligible rent**

The eligible rent is the amount the tenant pays to occupy their home; it does not include charges for heating, lighting, meals, water costs and service charges.

Any parts of the rent that the tenant does not have to pay to continue living in their home will not be included as part of the eligible rent.

The eligible rent is the amount that appears in the calculation of Housing Benefit and is called the Maximum Housing Benefit. The eligible rent is worked out in different ways depending on the type of tenancy.

**Income requirements**

If a tenant is in receipt of Income Support, Income-based Jobseeker's Allowance, Income-related Employment and Support Allowance (ESA) or the Guarantee Credit element of Pension Credit, Housing Benefit will cover all the **eligible rent,** subject to benefit cap restrictions.

**Savings Restrictions**

If a tenant has savings and/or investments the first £6000 of savings and investments is not considered when calculating a tenant's entitlement to Housing Benefit.

If the tenant has savings or investments of more

than £16,000 they will not be entitled to Housing Benefit or Council Tax Benefit.

## Capital Restrictions

If the tenant has over £16,000 in capital, they will not be eligible to claim Housing Benefit.

If the tenant or their partner has more than £16,000 in capital, they will not be entitled to receive Housing Benefit, unless they are in receipt of the Guarantee Credit element of Pension Credit.

## Change of Circumstances

Once a tenant is in receipt of housing benefit they have a duty to report any relevant change of circumstances to the Local Authority. E.g. change to income, new job, addition to the family, children starting full time work or staying on in higher education. Any request for further information must be provided to the Local Authority within 1 month, although a tenant can request an extension in time if they are experiencing any difficulties providing the requested information.

It is very important that the tenant reports any change of circumstances as soon as possible and obtains proof of reporting the change to the Local Authority e.g. a receipt for handing in documents, office visits. It is always preferable that a tenant attend in person rather than reporting a change of circumstances over the telephone so that the tenant can obtain proof of their visit.

If the tenant fails to report a change of circumstances and the Local Authority become aware of it later then they may have to repay any housing benefit that they have been overpaid.

## 7.3. Ineligibility for Housing benefit

A tenant will not be entitled to Housing Benefit in the following circumstances:

- If they live with, and must pay rent to, a close relative or in-law such as a parent, step-parent, son, daughter, stepson, step-daughter or their partners. However, the tenant may be eligible for housing benefit if they are renting property owned by a family member and following a detailed investigation into the tenancy by the Local Authority who will want to satisfy themselves that the tenancy is not a contrived tenancy (set up to take advantage of the housing benefit system) the tenant may be found eligible for housing benefit.

- To help with the costs of a mortgage or home loan.

- If the tenant is a full-time student, unless they have children or are disabled.

- If the tenant is an asylum seeker.

- If the tenant is under 35 they will only be eligible for housing benefit at the single room rate, the exceptions are care leavers under 22, those aged between 25-35 in homeless hostels, etc.

- The tenant does not have a right to reside (this will apply if the tenant is from a country in the European Union and they are not exercising treaty rights e.g. jobseeker, worker, self-employed, student or self-sufficient) or are subject to immigration control.

### 7.4. Local Housing Allowance

The Local Housing Allowance rates are used to calculate housing benefit for tenants renting from private landlords. The Local Housing Allowance rates depend on the area the tenant is making their claim in. These areas are called Broad Rental Market Areas (BRMA).

Under the Local Housing Allowance rules, housing benefit payments were capped in April 2012.
A tenant will be able to work out their entitlement to Housing Benefit based on the Local Housing Allowance rates using the following criteria:

To check the LHA rates a tenant will need:

- Details of how many people live in their household.

- If they are entitled to an additional bedroom for someone not living with them, but who provides necessary overnight care for them or their partner.

- The postcode of the property the tenant rents or wants to rent, or the Local Authority where the property is situated.

A tenant can work out their bedroom entitlement on the www.gov.uk website:

https://lhadirect.voa.gov.uk/BedRoomCalculator.aspx

If housing benefit does not pay the full rent due to the Local Housing Allowance rate cap the tenant must pay the shortfall in the rent to their landlord. If the tenant is unable to afford to pay the shortfall, then they can make an application for Discretionary Housing Benefit. Further information about Discretionary Housing Benefit can be found at Section 7.5.

## Unoccupied rooms (Bedroom tax)

From April 2013, if a council / social housing tenant has at least 1 extra bedroom in their house, their Housing Benefit could be reduced by:

- 14% of the 'eligible rent' if they have 1 extra bedroom.
- 25% of the 'eligible rent' if they have 2 or more extra bedrooms.

The reduction is worked out based on the tenant's eligible rent (including any eligible services). The new rules allow one bedroom for:

- Every adult couple (married or unmarried).

- Any other adult aged 16 or over.

- Any two children of the same sex aged under 16.

- Any two children aged under 10.

- Any other child (other than a foster child or child whose main home is elsewhere).

- A carer (or team of carers) who do not live with you but provide you or your partner with overnight care.

**Exemptions**

The new rules (bedroom tax) will not apply if:

- A tenant lives in 'supported accommodation' where the Local Authority provide or commission care.

- A tenant is a shared owner of the property.

- A tenant lives in temporary homeless accommodation.

- A sole tenant or both joint tenants are of 'pension credit age' (born 5/10/51 or before). If tenants were born after October 1951 or in early 1952, they will be affected, but only for a few months.

### 7.5. Discretionary Housing Benefit

Discretionary Housing Benefit is available for tenants who are in receipt of Housing Benefit but require further financial help with their housing costs.

An application for Discretionary Housing Benefit can be made by attending the Local Authority offices and making a written request.

There is no right of appeal against a refusal to award Discretionary Housing Benefit, however it may be possible to challenge the decision by way of a Judicial Review on public law grounds.

### 7.6. Challenging a Housing Benefit Decision

If a tenant wants to challenge a Housing Benefit decision because they disagree with the decision, they can ask for the decision to be looked at again by requesting a **review** or an **appeal** of the decision. A request for either a review and/or an appeal must be brought within one month from the date of the decision. If the decision has been looked at again following a request for a review and the tenant is not happy with the decision, the tenant may be able to appeal against the review decision.

If the tenant requests a review and/or appeal within one month and their review and/or appeal is successful, the decision will be changed from the date of the original decision.

If the tenant is unable to appeal within one month due to special circumstances e.g. they were in hospital, ill-health, bereavement, the housing benefit office may accept a late appeal. In a letter requesting an appeal the tenant will be required to explain the reasons for the late appeal in addition to providing reasons why they are appealing against the housing benefit decision. A late appeal can only be accepted within 13 months of the receipt of the decision letter.

**Appeal Procedure**

If the tenant appeals a Housing benefit decision

their appeal will be sent to an independent tribunal, called the First-Tier Tribunal at the HM Courts and Tribunals Service. The First-Tier Tribunal panel is made up of three individuals who will make an independent decision based on the law and the facts of the case.

Once the tenant's appeal has been received they will receive a form from HM Courts and Tribunal Service requesting that they provide further information on how they want the case to proceed and whether any special requirements need to be made. They will be required to return this form back to the HM Courts and Tribunal Service within 14 days.

The tenant will also be asked on the form if they want the appeal dealt with as an oral or paper hearing.

An oral hearing will take place at a set date and time within one of the First-Tier Tribunal Courts. The tenant will be required to attend (with/ without a representative) to put forward their submissions.

The tribunal will ask the tenant questions at the hearing and the tenant is permitted to submit supporting evidence. The tenant will be advised of the outcome of the hearing on the day.

A paper hearing means that the tribunal will consider all the evidence based on the papers that have been submitted. A hearing will not take place and the tenant will be notified of the decision by post.

If the tenant wants more details about the reasons for the decision and the tribunal's findings, they can request a statement of reasons from the tribunals within one month of the date of the decision.

If the tenant disagrees with the decision of the First-Tier Tribunal, they can only appeal the decision on a point of law e.g. if the First-Tier Tribunal has made an error in law/ misinterpreted the law. The point of law in dispute will be heard and decided by the Upper Tribunal.

# CHAPTER EIGHT

## Common Questions & Queries

**1. My landlord/letting agent has not renewed my tenancy agreement after the fixed term came to an end, what are my rights?**

Once the fixed term period ends the tenancy becomes a statutory periodic tenancy. The statutory periodic tenancy will continue on the same terms and conditions as the written tenancy. The period of the tenancy depends on the frequency of rent payments, i.e. If rent is paid monthly the tenancy will become a statutory periodic tenancy. The tenant retains all the rights they had when the fixed term period of the tenancy agreement was in effect. *Section 5 (2), Housing Act 1988.*

**2. My landlord has not provided me with a tenancy agreement, am I entitled to one?**

A tenancy agreement is not a legal requirement and a landlord will not be obligated to provide the tenant with one.

## 3. I do not have a tenancy agreement can I still claim Housing benefit?

The Housing benefit department can process a claim for housing benefit without a tenancy agreement. A tenant will be required to provide the housing benefit office with proof of rental liability to prove that they are contractually liable to pay rent. e.g. bank statements showing regular payments of rent to the landlord, a letter from the landlord confirming details of the tenancy agreement or a rent book.

## 4. My landlord has not provided me with a rent book?

A landlord is required by law to provide the tenant with a rent book or a similar document under *Section 4 and Section 5 Landlord and Tenant Act 1985.* The failure to provide the tenant with a rent book is a criminal (summary) offence and the landlord will be liable to receive a fine.

**Section 4, Landlord and Tenant Act 1985, Provision of rent books.**

(1)  Where a tenant has a right to occupy premises as a residence in consideration of a rent payable weekly, the landlord shall provide a rent book or other similar document for use in respect of the premises.

(2)  Subsection (1) does not apply to premises if the rent includes a payment in respect of board and the value of that board to the tenant forms a substantial proportion of the whole rent.

(3)  In this section and sections 5 to 7—
    (a)  "tenant" includes a statutory tenant and a person having a contractual right to occupy the premises; and
    (b)  "landlord", in relation to a person having such a contractual right, means the person who granted the right or any successor in title of his, as the case may require.

## Section 5 Information to be contained in rent books.

(1) A rent book or other similar document provided in pursuance of section 4 shall contain notice of the name and address of the landlord of the premises and—

   (a) if the premises are occupied by virtue of a restricted contract, particulars of the rent and of the other terms and conditions of the contract and notice of such other matters as may be prescribed;

   (b) if the premises are let on or subject to a protected or statutory tenancy *[or let on an assured tenancy within the meaning of Part I of the Housing Act 1988]*, notice of such matters as may be prescribed.

(2) If the premises are occupied by virtue of a restricted contract or let on or subject to a protected or statutory tenancy *[or let on an assured tenancy within the meaning of Part I*

of the Housing Act 1988], the notice and particulars required by this section shall be in the prescribed form.

(3) In this section "prescribed" means prescribed by regulations made by the Secretary of State, which—
   (a) may make different provision for different cases, and
   (b) shall be made by statutory instrument which shall be subject to annulment in pursuance of a resolution of either House of Parliament.

## 5. I do not know the name and address of my current landlord?

If a tenant requests the name and address of the landlord the landlord is legally required to provide the tenant with this information within 21 days. *Section 1 Landlord and Tenant Act 1985.*

**Landlord & Tenant Act 1985, Section 1**
*Information to be given to tenant*

(1) If the tenant of premises occupied as a dwelling makes a written request for the landlord's name and address to—

    (a) any person who demands, or the last person who received, rent payable under the tenancy, or

    (b) any other person for the time being acting as agent for the landlord, in relation to the tenancy, that person shall supply the tenant with a written statement of the landlord's name and address within the period of 21 days beginning with the day on which he receives the request.

(2) A person who, without reasonable excuse, fails to comply with subsection (1) commits a summary offence and is liable on conviction to a fine not exceeding level 4 on the standard scale.

(3) In this section and section 2—

    (a) "tenant" includes a statutory tenant; and

    (b) "landlord" means the immediate landlord.

The landlord must provide the tenant with their name and UK contact address further to *Section 47 and Section 48, Landlord and Tenant Act 1987*. Rent will not be due until the landlord has complied with *Section 47 and Section 48 of the Landlord and Tenant Act 1987*.

**Landlord and Tenant Act 1987, Section 47 Landlord's name and address to be contained in demands for rent etc.**

(1) *Where any written demand is given to a tenant of premises to which this Part applies, the demand must contain the following information, namely—*

    *(a) the name and address of the landlord, and*

> (b) *If that address is not in England and Wales, an address in England and Wales at which notices (including notices in proceedings) may be served on the landlord by the tenant.*

(2) *Where—*
> (a) *a tenant of any such premises is given such a demand, but*
> (b) *it does not contain any information required to be contained in it by virtue of subsection (1), then (subject to subsection (3)) any part of the amount demanded which consists of a service charge ("the relevant amount") shall be treated for all purposes as not being due from the tenant to the landlord at any time before that information is furnished by the landlord by notice given to the tenant.*

(3) *The relevant amount shall not be so treated in relation to any time when, by virtue of an order of any court, there is in force an*

*appointment of a receiver or manager whose functions include the receiving of service charges from the tenant.*

(4) *In this section "demand" means a demand for rent or other sums payable to the landlord under the terms of the tenancy.*

**Section 48 Notification by landlord of address for service of notices.**

(1) *A landlord of premises to which this Part applies shall by notice furnish the tenant with an address in England and Wales at which notices (including notices in proceedings) may be served on him by the tenant.*

(2) *Where a landlord of any such premises fails to comply with subsection (1), any rent or service charge otherwise due from the tenant to the landlord shall (subject to subsection (3)) be treated for all purposes as not being due from the tenant to the landlord at any time before the landlord does comply with*

*that subsection.*

*(3)    Any such rent or service charge shall not be so treated in relation to any time when, by virtue of an order of any court, there is in force an appointment of a receiver or manager whose functions include the receiving of rent or (as the case may be) service charges from the tenant.*

## 6. The white goods in my flat have broken down, does the landlord have to repair them?

The first point of reference for the tenant to check who is liable for repairing white goods will be the tenancy agreement. If the tenancy agreement is silent on who is responsible, then if the property is let with these items it will be implied that the landlord is responsible for repairing and/or replacing these items. It is generally accepted that landlords are responsible for maintaining any furniture, appliances or other items supplied as part of a furnished property for the benefit of the tenant. If it can be shown that the failure or damage has occurred through the tenant's negligence or other misuse, then the landlord will not be liable to carry out repairs/replacement. If the tenant has obtained their own white goods, then they will be responsible for the maintenance of these items.

## 7. My flat has a pest infestation, who is responsible?

The responsibility for remedying a pest infestation will depend on the following factors. 1) what the tenancy agreement says about pest infestation 2) Whether the property was infested with pests when the tenant moved in and 3) whether the infestation has resulted from an act or omission of the tenant.

The tenant should initially check the tenancy agreement to determine who is responsible for eradicating pests.

If the property is let as a furnished flat and pests are present when the tenant moves in the landlord has a contractual duty implied by common law to ensure that at the start of the tenancy the property is 'fit for habitation', this can include ensuring that the property is free from vermin infestation.

## When is the landlord responsible for dealing with pest infestation?

If the pest infestation was caused by a structural defect or disrepair which the landlord is responsible for remedying under *Section 11, Landlord & Tenant Act 1985* the landlord will be responsible for remedying the pest infestation.

The law states that some pests will be treated as a statutory nuisance but only if the pests are categorised as prejudicial to health. If the pest infestation is categorised as prejudicial to health and the tenant can show that the infestation is caused by the 'act, default or sufferance' of the landlord/agent, the tenant may be able to bring a prosecution under *Section 82 of the Environmental Protection Act 1990* if the landlord fails to do anything to abate the nuisance.

If the vermin do not constitute a statutory nuisance the tenant will be responsible for paying for pest control.

## When is the tenant responsible for dealing with pest infestation?

The tenant may be responsible for dealing with a pest infestation if they have done something or failed to do something which has caused the pest infestation.

## 8. Can I change the locks to the property to the exclusion of the landlord?

A tenant is not permitted to change the locks to the property to exclude the landlord. If the tenant does change the locks following a break-in/loss of keys they will have to provide the landlord with a copy of the keys if the landlord requires access in the event of an emergency. If a tenant's landlord is entering the property without the tenant's permission this is a trespass to property and the tenant should follow the procedure set out in the Step by Step Guide at Chapter 3.

## 9. Can the landlord increase the rent?

Different tenancies have different rules about when the landlord can increase the rent.

The rules for increasing the rent of Rent Act tenants is set out at Chapter 6.

When a Rent Act tenant receives notice of a rent increase from the landlord and upon receipt of this notice believes that the rent increase is unfair, they can apply to the First Tier Tribunal (Property Chamber- Residential Property) Rent Property Tribunal who will decide what the fair rent should be.

The rent increases for Secure and Assured tenants are imposed by the Local Authority/Housing Association and take place every April. The rent increases are made in line with inflation and the RPI Index.

A tenant of an assured short hold tenancy will have their rent increased in the following ways:

If the tenancy is still within the **fixed term** the landlord cannot increase the rent unless the tenancy agreement states that the landlord can increase the rent or the tenant agrees to the increase. If the landlord grants the tenant a new fixed term tenancy, then the landlord can increase the rent as per the terms of the new tenancy agreement. If the tenant does not agree to the rent increase in the new tenancy agreement and refuses to sign the agreement, the new rent will not be enforceable and the landlord will have to undertake possession proceedings to obtain possession of the property.

Once the fixed term of a tenancy has come to an end and a new agreement has not been signed, the tenancy automatically becomes a **periodic tenancy**. A landlord can increase the rent after the first fixed term of the tenancy in the following circumstances:

- The tenancy agreement contains information on the procedure for a rent increase.

- The landlord gives the tenant the required notice of the intended rent increase. (Section 13 Notice).

- The landlord provides the tenant with written notice that a change will be made to the terms of the tenancy agreement. (Section 6 Notice).

- The landlord and tenant agree on a rent increase.

The landlord will have to follow the correct statutory procedure to increase the rent if the tenancy agreement makes no mention of a rent increase and/ or the landlord and tenant do not agree on a rent increase.

The correct statutory procedure is set out below:

**Section 13 Notice procedure**

A landlord is required to serve the tenant with a Section 13 Notice (*Section 13(2) Housing Act 1988*) which will provide the tenant with notice that the landlord intends to increase the rent.

- For a monthly, weekly or fortnightly tenancy one month's notice of the intended increase is required.

- For a yearly tenancy, a period of six months' notice is required before the increase can be put into effect.

The date on which the new rent is required must not be earlier than a year after the date when the rent was last increased using a Section 13 notice. If a new tenancy is in place, then the date should not be any earlier than a year after the date when the tenancy started.

The landlord will have to comply with *Section 13, Housing Act 1988* and serve notice of the rent increase using the prescribed form. If the landlord does not follow the correct procedure the rent increase will be unlawful, and the new rent will be unenforceable.

## Section 6 Notice procedure

Once the periodic tenancy commences the landlord (or tenant) can serve a notice under Section 6, Housing Act 1988 proposing new tenancy terms including an increase in the rent.

## Challenging a rent increase

A tenant can challenge a rent increase in the following ways:

- If a tenant thinks that the rent charged on the property is excessively high they can refer the rent to the First Tier Tribunal (Property Chamber- Residential Property) within the first six months of the fixed term of the tenancy, (*Section 14, Housing Act 1988*). However, after the initial fixed term period, and once the tenant has signed a new agreement, they will no longer be able to refer the rent to the Tribunal.

- If a landlord serves the tenant with a Section 13 Notice (*Section 13, Housing Act 1988*), the tenant can request a rent review by applying to the First Tier Tribunal (Property Chamber- Residential Property) before the new rent is due to commence and within 1 month of the new rent being introduced.

- If a landlord or a tenant serves a Section 6 Notice (*Section 6, Housing Act 1988*) the landlord or the tenant can request a rent review by applying to the First Tier Tribunal (Property Chamber- Residential Property) within the period of three months beginning on the date on which the notice was served on him.

- The tenant will not be entitled to refer the matter to the First Tier Tribunal (Property Chamber-Residential Property) if the Tribunal have already determined what the rent for the current term of the tenancy should be or six months have elapsed since the start of the tenancy. (*Section 22, Housing Act 1988 as amended by Section 100 Housing Act 1988*).

The deadlines for appealing to the tribunal depend on the type of tenancy that the tenant has:

- If the tenancy is an assured or assured shorthold tenancy, the tenant is required to appeal before the new rent is due to start.

- If the tenancy is a Rent Act 'regulated tenancy' and a fair rent has been set by a Rent Valuation Officer the tenant can appeal against the fair rent that has been set within 28 days of the rent being decided by the Rent Valuation Officer.

The Rent Property Tribunal has the power to lower the rent, set it at the same level or increase the rent. When the new rent is set by a Rent Valuation Officer it will be fixed for one year.

### 10. Can I end the tenancy during the fixed term period?

If the tenant ends the tenancy during the fixed term period, the tenant will remain liable for the rent that remains due for the remainder of the fixed term period of the tenancy.

The tenant can attempt to reach an agreement with the landlord to surrender the tenancy with no liability for the rest of the rental period, however if the landlord is not agreeable to this the tenant should attempt to find a replacement tenant to assume the rental liability for the remaining duration of the tenancy agreement. Tenants are advised to either request a break clause in the tenancy or request a six-month tenancy should they wish to end the tenancy.

## 11. I only have an oral agreement, what are my rights?

A tenant who has an oral agreement has the same rights as a tenant who has signed a written tenancy agreement. The main tenancy rights can be summarised as follows: the right to occupy the property to the exclusion of all others, the landlord must follow the correct legal procedure to obtain possession of the property, the landlord is required to undertake repairs to the property as implied by Section 11, Landlord & Tenant Act 1985 and the landlord must follow the correct legal procedure to increase the rent.

# CHAPTER NINE
# Legal Aid

## 9.1. Legal Aid: Legal advice and representation

The Legal Aid Agency provide civil and criminal legal aid advice and representation in England & Wales.

Legal Aid is available from legal aid providers for those who are in receipt of benefits or a low income, Solicitors who have a contract with the Legal Aid Agency will be permitted to take on cases that are in scope for legal aid.

Legal Aid will only be available for some housing cases as set out below (subject to the tenant being financially eligible).

Legal aid is available for the following type of housing cases:
1. Possession Proceedings
2. Harassment and Illegal Eviction
3. Homelessness

4. Disrepair which poses a serious risk of harm to the health or safety of the tenant or the tenant's family who occupy the property.

## **Financial Eligibility**

A tenant will automatically qualify for Legal Aid if:

- They are directly in receipt of a Passporting Benefit
- Gross income does not exceed £2657.00 per month
- Disposable income does not exceed £733.00 per month
- Disposable capital not to exceed £8000.00 (for civil cases).

Clients in receipt of the following passporting benefit will be automatically eligible for legal aid subject to assessment of their capital.

The following benefits are passported benefits:

- Income Support

- Income Related Employment and Support (ESA)
- Income based Jobseekers Allowance (JSA)
- Universal credit
- Guaranteed State Pension Credit
- Payments from NASS in respect of Immigration and Asylum.

If a tenant is employed their gross income cannot exceed £2,657.00 (If the tenant has more than 4 dependent children, £222.00 can be added to this figure for the fifth child and each further child). After permitted deductions the tenant cannot have a disposable income of more than £733.00 per month. The tenant's capital cannot exceed £8000.00.

A tenant can check their financial eligibility using the civil legal aid eligibility calculator: www.civil-eligibility-calculator.justice.gov.uk

**Housing cases**

Legal aid is available for the following type of housing cases:

5. Possession Proceedings
6. Harassment and Illegal Eviction
7. Homelessness
8. Disrepair which poses a serious risk of harm to the health or safety of the tenant or the tenant's family who occupy the property.

A tenant can find a Legal Aid Solicitor in their area using the link below:
www.legaladviserfinder.justice.gov.uk/AdviserSearch.do

A tenant can obtain legal advice for family, debt, benefits, housing, education or employment problems, by contacting Civil Legal Advice:

Telephone: 0845 345 4 345
Minicom: 0845 609 6677
Monday to Friday: 9am to 8pm
Saturday: 9am to 12:30pm

A tenant can also text 'legalaid' and their name to 80010 to get a call back. The cost is the same as a normal text message.

# ANNEXE

## **Annex 1**

**TENANCY AGREEMENT**
**ASSURED SHORTHOLD TENANCY**
**governed by the Housing Act 1988 as amended by the Housing Act 1996**

DATE:

PARTIES:

1. (The Landlord/s):

2. (The Tenant/s):

PROPERTY ADDRESS:

TERM (length of the tenancy):
The tenancy is granted for a fixed term of……………………
months/years
From: (start date)
To: (end date)

And thereafter on a (weekly/monthly/ quarterly/six monthly/annual) periodic tenancy

RENT: £                              per (week//month/quarter/six-month/annual)

Payable in advance by equal (insert period..........................)
payments on the ...............................day of each (insert
period .......................)

First payment to be made on the ................................

DEPOSIT: A deposit of £         is payable on signing this agreement.

1.  The Landlord agrees to let and the Tenant agrees to take the Property and contents for the term at the rent payable as above.

2.  The Tenant pays the deposit to the landlord as security for the performance of the tenant's obligations.

3.  The Tenant agrees with the Landlord: -
    To pay the rent as set out above.

4.  The Tenant is solely liable for the payment of all charges for the supply of utilities (such as electricity, gas, water and telephone), in respect of the accommodation during the period of the tenancy. The tenant will take all reasonable steps to transfer such utilities into his/her name. The tenant must not seek, or allow, or disconnection of any utility, or alter the identity of the supplier without the prior written permission of the landlord. The tenant will be liable for

the cost of the reconnection of any of these services.

5. The Tenant is responsible for keeping the interior of the property, the internal decorations, fixtures and fittings and appliances in the property in good repair and condition (except damage caused by accidental fire and except for anything that the Landlord is responsible to repair under this agreement or by statute).

6. To allow the Landlord/Landlords agent to enter the property to inspect the condition of the property and carry out repairs at reasonable times upon furnishing the Tenant with 24 hours' notice beforehand.

7. To use the property as their sole and principal home and not sublet the property to any third party.

8. Not to do or allow anyone else to do anything on the Property which may cause a nuisance, damage or annoyance to the tenants or occupiers of the adjoining premises.

9. Not to assign or sublet the Property and not to part with possession of the Property in any other way without the Landlord's consent.

10. If the tenant -
Is at least fourteen days late paying rent, or any part of it, whether or not the Rent has been formally

demanded, or has broken any of the terms of the agreement then subject to any statutory provisions, the Landlord may recover possession of the Property and the tenancy will come to an end. Any other rights or remedies the Landlord may have will remain in force

11. The Landlord has an obligation under s11 Landlord and Tenant Act 1985 to keep in repair the structure and exterior of the dwelling house, including drains, gutters and external pipes; and to keep in repair and proper working order the installations for the supply of water, gas and electricity for sanitation (including basins, sinks and baths and sanitary conveniences) and for space heating and heating water. The landlord is not obligated to repair until the tenant has given notice of the defect, and the tenant is obligated to take proper care of the Property and to do small jobs which a reasonable tenant would **do).**

**NOTICE OF LANDLORD'S ADDRESS**

The Landlord notifies the Tenant that notices can be served on the Landlord by the tenant at the following address:

This notice is given under section 48 of the Landlord and Tenant Act 1987, if applicable. The address must be in England & Wales.

As witnessed by the parties on the date specified below

Signed by the above named
The Landlord in the presence of

Signed by the above named (Tenant)
In the presence of:

## Annex 2

FORM 3

# Notice seeking possession of a property let on an Assured Tenancy or an Assured Agricultural Occupancy

Housing Act 1988 section 8 as amended by section 151 of the Housing Act 1996, section 97 of the Anti-social Behaviour, Crime and Policing Act 2014, and section 41 of the Immigration Act 2016.

- Please write clearly in black ink.
- Please cross out text marked with an asterisk (*) that does not apply.
- This form should be used where possession of accommodation let under an assured tenancy, an assured agricultural occupancy or an assured shorthold tenancy is sought on one of the grounds in Schedule 2 to the Housing Act 1988.
- Do not use this form if possession is sought on the "shorthold" ground under section 21 of the Housing Act 1988 from an assured shorthold tenant where the fixed term has come to an end or, for assured shorthold tenancies with no fixed term which started on or after 28th February 1997, after six months has elapsed. Form 6A 'Notice seeking possession of a property let on an Assured Shorthold Tenancy' is prescribed for these cases.

1    To................................................................................

Name(s) of tenant(s)/licensee(s)*

2    Your landlord/licensor* intends to apply to the court for an order requiring you to give up possession of....................

........................................................................................

..............................................................

*Address of premises*

3   Your landlord/licensor* intends to seek possession on ground(s) ..........in Schedule 2 to the Housing Act 1988 (as amended), which read (s)
..............................................................
..............................................................
..............................................................

*Give the full text (as set out in the Housing Act 1988 (as amended) of each ground which is being relied on. Continue on a separate sheet if necessary.*

4   Give a full explanation of why each ground is being relied on: ..................................................................
..............................................................
..............................................................
..............................................................

*Continue on a separate sheet if necessary.*

**Notes on the grounds for possession**

- If the court is satisfied that any of grounds 1 to 8 is established, it must make an order (but see below in respect of fixed term tenancies).

- Before the court will grant an order on any of grounds 9 to 17, it must be satisfied that it is reasonable to require you to leave. This means that, if one of these grounds is set out in section 3, you will be able to suggest to the court that it is not reasonable that you should have to leave, even if you accept that the ground applies.

- The court will not make an order under grounds 1, 3 to 6[1], 9 or 16, to take effect during the fixed

---

[1] Amended to reflect changes shortly to be made to correct the form prescribed in the Assured Tenancies and Agricultural Occupancies (Forms) (England) Regulations 2015.

As witnessed by the parties on the date specified below

Signed by the above named
The Landlord in the presence of

Signed by the above named (Tenant)
In the presence of:

demanded, or has broken any of the terms of the agreement then subject to any statutory provisions, the Landlord may recover possession of the Property and the tenancy will come to an end. Any other rights or remedies the Landlord may have will remain in force

11. The Landlord has an obligation under s11 Landlord and Tenant Act 1985 to keep in repair the structure and exterior of the dwelling house, including drains, gutters and external pipes; and to keep in repair and proper working order the installations for the supply of water, gas and electricity for sanitation (including basins, sinks and baths and sanitary conveniences) and for space heating and heating water. The landlord is not obligated to repair until the tenant has given notice of the defect, and the tenant is obligated to take proper care of the Property and to do small jobs which a reasonable tenant would **do).**

**NOTICE OF LANDLORD'S ADDRESS**

The Landlord notifies the Tenant that notices can be served on the Landlord by the tenant at the following address:

This notice is given under section 48 of the Landlord and Tenant Act 1987, if applicable. The address must be in England & Wales.

term of the tenancy (if there is one) and it will only make an order during the fixed term on grounds 2, 7, 7A, 8, 10 to 15 or 17 if the terms of the tenancy make provision for it to be brought to an end on any of these grounds. It may make an order for possession on ground 7B during a fixed-term of the tenancy even if the terms of the tenancy do not make provision for it to be brought to an end on this ground.

- Where the court makes an order for possession solely on ground 6 or 9, the landlord must pay your reasonable removal expenses.

5   The court proceedings will not begin until after:
......................................................................................
......................................................................................

*Give the earliest date on which court proceedings can be brought*

**Notes on the earliest date on which court proceedings can be brought**

- Where the landlord is seeking possession on grounds 1, 2, 5 to 7, 9 or 16 (without ground 7A or 14), court proceedings cannot begin earlier than 2 months from the date this notice is served on you and not before the date on which the tenancy (had it not been assured) could have been brought to an end by a notice to quit served at the same time as this notice. This applies even if one of grounds 3, 4, 7B, 8, 10 to 13, 14ZA, 14A, 15 or 17 is also specified.

- Where the landlord is seeking possession on grounds 3, 4, 7B, 8, 10 to 13, 14ZA, 14A, 15 or 17 (without ground 7A or 14), court proceedings cannot begin earlier than 2 weeks from the date this notice is served. If one of 1, 2, 5 to 7, 9 or 16 grounds is also specified court proceedings cannot begin earlier than two months from the date this notice is served.

- Where the landlord is seeking possession on ground 7A (with or without other grounds), court proceedings cannot begin earlier than 1 month from the date this notice is served on you and not before the date on which the tenancy (had it not been assured) could have been brought to an end by a notice to quit served at the same time as this notice. A notice seeking possession on ground 7A must be served on you within specified time periods which vary depending on which condition is relied upon:

- Where the landlord proposes to rely on condition 1, 3 or 5: within 12 months of the conviction (or if the conviction is appealed: within 12 months of the conclusion of the appeal);
- Where the landlord proposes to rely on condition 2: within 12 months of the court's finding that the injunction has been breached (or if the finding is appealed: within 12 months of the conclusion of the appeal);
- Where the landlord proposes to rely on condition 4: within 3 months of the closure order (or if the order is appealed: within 3 months of the conclusion of the appeal).

- Where the landlord is seeking possession on ground 14 (with or without other grounds other than ground 7A), court proceedings cannot begin before the date this notice is served.

- Where the landlord is seeking possession on ground 14A, court proceedings cannot begin unless the landlord has served, or has taken all reasonable steps to serve, a copy of this notice on the partner who has left the property.

- After the date shown in section 5, court proceedings may be begun at once but not later than 12 months from the date on which this notice is served. After this time the notice will lapse and a new notice must be served before possession can be sought.

6   Name and address of landlord/licensor*.

*To be signed and dated by the landlord or licensor or the landlord's or licensor's agent (someone acting for the landlord or licensor). If there are joint landlords each landlord or the agent must sign unless one signs on behalf of the rest with their agreement.*

*Signed* ...................................................................

*Date* ....................................................................

*Please specify whether:* landlord / licensor / joint landlords / landlord's agent

*Name(s) (Block Capitals)* .........................................
................................................................................

*Address* ................................................................
................................................................................
................................................................................

*Telephone*: Daytime ...............................................
Evening....................................................................

## What to do if this notice is served on you

- This notice is the first step requiring you to give up possession of your home. You should read it very carefully.

- Your landlord cannot make you leave your home without an order for possession issued by a court. By issuing this notice your landlord is informing you that he intends to seek such an order. If you are willing to give up possession without a court order, you should tell the person who signed this notice as soon as possible and say when you are prepared to leave.

- Whichever grounds are set out in section 3 of this form, the court may allow any of the other grounds to be added at a later date. If this is done, you will be told about it so you can discuss the additional grounds at the court hearing as well as the grounds set out in section 3.

- If you need advice about this notice, and what you should do about it, take it immediately to a citizens' advice bureau, a housing advice centre, a law centre or a solicitor.

## **Annex 3**

# NOTICE TO QUIT

## (BY LANDLORD OF PREMISES LET AS A DWELLING)

| | |
|---|---|
| Name and address of tenant | TO: of: |
| Name and address of Landlord | [I] [We] [as] [on behalf of] your landlord ......... Of ................................................................................. ................................................................................. |
| Delete as appropriate | give you NOTICE TO QUIT and deliver up possession to me/them* |
| Address of Premises | Of* ............................................................................... ................................................................................. |
| *Date for of Tenancy Possession | On*......20......... or the day on which a complete period the tenancy expires next after the end of four weeks from service of this notice. |
| Date of notice | Dated.....................20............................. Signed................................................................ |
| Name and address of Agent if Agent serves notice | ................................................................... |

## INFORMATION FOR TENANTS

*(See Note 2 below)*

1. If the tenant or licensee does not leave the dwelling, the landlord or licensor must give an order for possession from the court before the tenant or licensee can lawfully be evicted. The landlord or licensor cannot apply for such an order before the notice to quit or notice to determine has run out.

2. A tenant or licensee who does not know if he has any right to remain in possession after a notice to quit or a notice to determine runs out can obtain advice from a solicitor. Help with all or part of the cost of legal advice and assistance may be available under the Legal Aid Scheme. He should also be able to obtain information from a Citizens Advice Bureau, a Law Centre or a Housing Officer.

**NOTES**

1. Notice to quit premises let as a dwelling must be given at least four weeks before it takes effect, and it must be in writing (Protection from Eviction Act 1977, s.5 as amended.

2. Where a notice to quit is given by a landlord to determine a tenancy of any premises let as a dwelling, the notice must give this information (The Notices to Quit etc. (Prescribed Information) Regulations 1988).

3. Some tenancies are excluded from this protection:

See Protection from Eviction Act 1977, ss.3A and 5 (1B).

# Annex 4

**FORM 6A Notice seeking possession of a property let on an Assured Shorthold Tenancy**

Housing Act 1988 section 21(1) and (4) as amended by section 194 and paragraph 103 of Schedule 11 to the Local Government and Housing Act 1989 and section 98(2) and (3) of the Housing Act 1996

Please write clearly in black ink. Please tick boxes where appropriate.

This form should be used where a no fault possession of accommodation let under an assured shorthold tenancy (AST) is sought under section 21(1) or (4) of the Housing Act 1988.

There are certain circumstances in which the law says that you cannot seek possession against your tenant using section 21 of the Housing Act 1988, in which case you should not use this form.

These are:
(a) during the first four months of the tenancy (but where the tenancy is a replacement tenancy, the four-month period is calculated by reference to the start of the original tenancy and not the start of the replacement tenancy – see section 21(4B) of the Housing Act 1988);

(b) where the landlord is prevented from retaliatory eviction under section 33 of the Deregulation Act 2015;

(c) where the landlord has not provided the tenant with an energy performance certificate, gas safety certificate or the Department for Communities and Local Government's publication "How to rent: the checklist for renting in England" (see the Assured Shorthold Tenancy Notices and Prescribed Requirements (England) Regulations 2015);

(d) where the landlord has not complied with the tenancy deposit protection legislation; or

(e) where a property requires a licence but is unlicensed.

Landlords who are unsure about whether they are affected by these provisions should seek specialist advice.

This form must be used for all ASTs created on or after 1 October 2015 except for statutory periodic tenancies which have come into being on or after 1 October 2015 at the end of fixed term ASTs created before 1 October 2015. There is no obligation to use this form in relation to ASTs created prior to 1 October 2015, however it may nevertheless be used for all ASTs.

**What to do if this notice is served on you**

You should read this notice very carefully. It explains that your landlord has started the process to regain possession of the property referred to in section 2 below.

You are entitled to at least two months' notice before being required to give up possession of the property. However, if your tenancy started on a periodic basis without any initial fixed term a longer notice period may be required depending on how often you are required to pay rent (for example, if you pay rent quarterly, you must be given at least three months' notice, or, if you have a periodic tenancy which is half yearly or annual, you must be given at least six months' notice (which is the maximum)). The date you are required to leave should be shown in section 2 below. After this date the landlord can apply to court for a possession order against you.

Where your tenancy is terminated before the end of a period of your tenancy (e.g. where you pay rent in advance on the first of each month and you are required to give up possession in the middle of the month), you may be entitled to repayment of rent from the landlord under section 21C of the Housing Act 1988.

If you need advice about this notice, and what you should do about it, take it immediately to a citizens' advice bureau, a housing advice centre, a law centre or a solicitor.

1. To: Name(s) of tenant(s) (Block Capitals)

2. You are required to leave the below address after [            ]1. If you do not leave, your landlord may apply to the court for an order under section 21(1) or (4) of the Housing Act 1988 requiring you to give up possession.

Address of premises

---

1 Landlords should insert a calendar date here. The date should allow sufficient time to ensure that the notice is properly served on the tenant(s). This will depend on the method of service being used and landlords should check whether the tenancy agreement makes specific provision about service. Where landlords are seeking an order for possession on a periodic tenancy under section 21(4) of the Housing Act 1988, the notice period should also not be shorter than the period of the tenancy (up to a maximum of six months), e.g. where there is a quarterly periodic tenancy, the date should be three months from the date of service.

3. This notice is valid for six months only from the date of issue unless you have a periodic tenancy under which more than two months' notice is required (see notes accompanying this form) in which case this notice is valid for four months only from the date specified in section 2 above.

4. Name and address of landlord

*To be signed and dated by the landlord or their agent (someone acting for them). If there are joint landlords each landlord or the agent should sign unless one signs on behalf of the rest with their agreement.*

Signed                                    Date (DD/MM/YYYY)

[ ]                                       [ ]

Please specify whether:      landlord        joint landlords
landlord's agent

Name(s) of signatory/signatories (Block Capitals)

[ ]

[ ]

Address(es) of signatory/signatories

[ ]

Telephone of signatory/signatories

Printed in Great Britain
by Amazon